TITS AND TEETH
IN THAILAND

Billy Makin

KBO Authors

CONTENTS

Title Page

Copyright

TITS AND TEETH IN THAILAND

Guarding the empire   1

A SOMEWHAT CHEQUERED PAST   3

Chapter 1   4

Chapter 2   10

Chapter 3   17

Chapter 4   24

Chapter 5   27

Chapter 6   33

Chapter 7   41

Chapter 8   45

Chapter 9   54

Chapter 10   58

Chapter 11   67

Chapter 12   76

Chapter 13   80

Chapter 14   84

Chapter 15   90

Chapter 16   95

Chapter 17   101

Chapter 18   108

Chapter 19   118

Chapter 20   124

Chapter 21   130

Chapter 22   135

Chapter 23   143

Chapter 24   150

Chapter 25   155

Chapter 26   162

Chapter 27   169

Chapter 28   175

Chapter 29   182

Chapter 30   187

Chapter 31   191

Chapter 32   197

Chapter 33   202

Chapter 34   206

Chapter 35   209

Chapter 36   212

Chapter 37   217

Chapter 38   222

Monty is still in the saddle   223

Would you please consider leaving a review?   225

Books by Billy Makin   226

THE AUTHOR   228

Books by Billy Makin   231

TITS AND TEETH
IN THAILAND

Billy Makin

www.billymakin.com
Enquiries: admin@kboauthors.com

GUARDING THE EMPIRE

In my army days, at her Majesty's personal request.

A long, long time ago in Singapore.

'Let's get married.' said Rinda.

'When we get to know each other a little better.'
said Billy. 'Eight years is much too early.'

A SOMEWHAT CHEQUERED PAST

From university to accountant.

From soldier to engineer.

From fishing float manufacturer to commercial fishery owner.

From retiree to Thai bar owner, beer taster, and bar girl trainer.

From author to Lothario.

Is this the final testing ground and resting place for Monty?

Will he survive the relentless sexual advances
of 100,000 Pattaya bar girls?

Will the world's supply of Viagra be enough?

Where did it all go wrong Billy?

CHAPTER 1
ARRIVAL

"You want nice girl mister?"

I looked down at the dishevelled creature talking to me and wondered why so many flies were buzzing around him.

"She have nice tits and teeth."

I tried to respond but the sleeping tablets still had me in their grip.

"She bum-bum you long time mister."

"You after a punch on the nose?" I was indignant. "I'm not a poof so sod off."

I had been warned about Thai ladyboys, and despite my suffering from sleep deprivation, Mike Tyson wouldn't have been able to get into the private and well-guarded place that this perverted, slightly whiffy cretin was suggesting.

"She velly good mister, she my sister."

I had been travelling for what seemed like days; from Tenerife to Heathrow, and then on to Dubai followed by Thailand. I had left the plane no more than one hour earlier here in Bangkok airport and some hairy arsed dwarf, his armpits and clothes smelling like a badger's bum, wanted to know if I would like to pay for the privilege of having a ladyboy stick something up my bottom.

I had a lot to learn about Thailand and was already out of my depth.

Quite innocently I had read the bum-bum phrase wrong, it is in fact boom-boom, and is simply pronounced differently over here; the meaning for those of you who have never been to the sex capital of the world being a jolly good rogering, or for the more refined of us, the act of copulation in order to maintain a stable population, OK then, fill in the missing letters if you must ------g.

Shame on you.

Having been in Thailand for a little over 8 years now, it is difficult to comprehend why the country has in fact got less people than China, as boom-boom is not only the national sport, it is also a national obsession, right up there with eating and money.

A fairly stable population density is largely maintained by the number of births only slightly exceeding the number of road deaths. To drive on Thailand's roads is the wheeled equivalent of playing Russian roulette with 5 loaded bullets and one empty chamber, only with considerably lower survival odds. Thailand has in fact got the worst road statistics in the world.

I sat on the bus to Pattaya, the one-and-a-half-hour journey costing no more than a fiver and found myself talking Thai-glish to an extremely pretty girl called Lek, who appeared to be around 18 and was returning from Korea.

Monty awoke from a deep sleep, and forgetting that he was supposed to be sulking, suddenly took an interest in the conversation.

I was pleased for him; Monty had been my lifelong friend since birth and had attracted much attention in the maternity ward once the midwife had finished spanking me. I never worked out what I had done wrong as I was barely 5 seconds old.

Thai girls often look considerably younger than their true age, and as she was dressed in a micro-skirt and a low-cut blouse, neither Monty nor I were paying too much attention to her face.

Her frankness took me quite by surprise as she explained that she had been to Seoul, the South Korean capital for a couple of weeks to see one of her numerous foreign boyfriends, and proudly proclaimed that her sexual exploits had earned her quite a bit of money.

"One of your boyfriends?" I was puzzled.

"Oh yes, I have many boyfriends, I boom-boom lots of men and soon I buy house for my Mama." She paused for a few seconds before continuing. "I like Farang men best, Thai and Korea men only have small dickie."

Monty, my ever-present pet python was listening in to the conversation and was beginning to stir in my loins, excitedly and quite noticeably, my shorts suddenly becoming a little tight.

Monty has always been a bit of a womanizer ever since my goolies dropped, especially since moving to Thailand, and has acquired the embarrassing habit of sticking his nose into any conversation I may be having with the female of the species; the younger and prettier the girl, the more notice he appears to take. However, it has been observed that his vision becomes somewhat clouded and his judgement questionable when he has been out drinking with me.

The journey flew by, and with each passing mile, Monty and I realized that together we were both going to enjoy Pattaya very much indeed, starting with tomorrow night. I now had directions to Lek's bar and had arranged to meet her at eight in the evening; the golf would have to wait, I had more important fish to fry.

We
meet
again
Lek

I continued to feel occasional pangs of guilt throughout the journey.

I was now approaching the mythical and oft denied point between middle and old age and was due to embark on a new life, a life that I hadn't really prepared for. Somehow, I had always imagined that Sandra and I would live happily ever after before riding off into the sunset together, after all, we had been together for many years.

One day, completely out of the blue she told me that she needed a little space.

I knew that we had come to the end of the road; I had seen it coming for months but had refused to accept it.

How the hell could any girl NOT want to live with me for God's sake?

Monty had been equally devastated at the news; it broke my heart when I had to tell him, and up until the bus journey with Lek he had been sulking for days on end, refusing to even show his face unless the lights had been switched off.

On yer bike Billy boy

"Is 7,000 miles enough space?" I had said bravely, in fact flippantly, trying to hide the pain.

That was why I was now on the bus to Pattaya, and despite both mind and body feeling completely shattered, Monty continued to remind me of the delights that lay ahead the next evening.

Lek was in fact 25 years old and gave me a rather uplifting kiss once we had left the bus at the Pattaya bus station, both Monty and I waving goodbye as she climbed onto a motorbike taxi.

A taxi pulled up alongside me, the driver reeking of cheap Thai whisky. "Do you know the way to the Diana Inn?" I asked.

"Yes boss, jump in, 500 baht."

The 10-minute-high speed suicidal joy ride through the crowded Pattaya streets became a nightmare, my driver laughing at every near miss as motorbikes and cabs jostled for space that wasn't even there. I was damned pleased when I eventually climbed out of the Toyota cab.

I handed over the 500 baht, the driver shooting off like a scalded cat.

For some strange reason, the place felt familiar – almost a Deja vu experience. The sign on the hotel said "Diana Inn," and across the road was the sign "Bus Station."

The bastard had just charged me a tenner in English money to take me across the road.

As always, Monty mocked.

I threatened him with a cold shower.

He shut up.

I had a lot to learn about Thailand.

CHAPTER 2
SETTLING IN

Having checked in at the hotel, I walked to my room, showered, and slumped into bed totally shattered.

My dreams took me back to the life and wife that I had left behind.

Should I have tried harder to make it work or should I have manfully walked away once I realized that it was going nowhere? I had spent too many months in limbo refusing to let go – terrified of leaving my comfort zone.

I awoke with a start at the banging on the door.

"Hi, I'm Andy from the room next door," the cheery voice said as I opened the door completely starkers; Monty was noticeably still fast asleep. "We've got a bit of a party on downstairs tonight and you are more than welcome to join us."

I thanked him and agreed to be there, before suddenly realizing that I hadn't eaten for hours. I had managed an overpriced burger at Dubai, but thanks to the sleeping pills had slept throughout the 6-hour journey to Bangkok.

I vaguely remembered a small cafe by the bus station where that cheating taxi bastard had picked me up, so I dressed and made the 500 baht walk all the way across the road and into the open wooden shack that masqueraded as a cafe.

The handwritten menu was all in Thai, so I simply pointed to something halfway down the listing. "You like spicy?" The voice was that of an extremely pretty, young girl of about 14. "Yes please," I replied, "very spicy."

Now before I go any further, I must point out that in both Spain and the UK, the word spicy is taken to mean lots of spicy flavours, in Thailand however, it means what we would term as hot, i.e. with lots of chillies.

Within minutes, the most appalling mix of fish, meat and rice appeared in what I can only describe as a bowl of hot, dirty, dishwater.

"Ah well," I thought. "When in Rome."

I closed my eyes and rammed in a spoonful of what is best described as dog shit flavoured rocket fuel.

Just light the blue touch paper

It nearly blew the top of my head off, at which point, if I had had a gun in my hand, I WOULD have blown the top of my head off to relieve the pain.

The first bottle of iced water disappeared, and as the young girl was watching me with some amusement, I somehow had to manfully soldier on.

She walked over to me with another bottle of water and gently stroked my neck before leaving.

Together with 4 more bottles of iced water, and with considerable relief, I finally and triumphantly finished the toxic concoction known as Thai food.

The owner of the bar sauntered over with a smug look on her face. "You like?" She said.

Not wishing to tell her that a frantic sexual liaison with a rabid porcupine would have been preferable, I stupidly nodded, before downing yet another bottle of water.

"For you, only 500 baht, she have great tits and teeth." she said.

I was confused as the menu had only said 50 baht.

Again she spoke. "Only 500-baht, food free."

She then pointed at the young girl. "She my daughter, she velly good, she love you long time."

She love you long time Garry

"Bloody hell," I said, standing up as I spoke. "I'm not Garry Glitter."

"OK Garry," she went on. "For you, I give special price, only 300 baht. You bring home morning for school."

I handed over 100 baht and swiftly moved on to the party back at the hotel, this time saving the 500-baht taxi fare by walking across the road.

The beer was good – the girls were possibly even better, and several bottles of Tiger beer later I began to feel a little wobbly.

Strange noises were bubbling and rumbling deep in my innards.

Monty, who had taken a fancy to a pretty, little candy bar called Pom went berserk when I dragged him away from her, made my apologies and disappeared upstairs, where I immediately retired to bed, dreaming of Lek and the gymnastics that would be waiting for me just around the corner the following evening.

I would guess that it was around 6 in the morning, just as the sun was coming up that I awoke from a deeply erotic sleep.

I immediately knew that I was in trouble.

I clenched the cheeks of my aris with enough force to crack a walnut and made a life-or-death dash for the toilet.

Just in time, with no more than a second to spare, I hit the pan, accompanied by an explosion that made Krakatoa seem like a very small firework. The resulting volcanic eruption and percussion wave slammed the toilet door closed and almost shot the wax out of my ears.

ONE SECOND TO SPARE

My aris began to warm.

Within seconds someone was pouring molten lead into it.

Volcanic aris syndrome

Splashing water from the sink did not work, and so the next half hour found me under the shower, on my knees, prostrated in the Muslim prayer position with the cold water running between my cheeks.

I needed a pee.

Monty was horrified and pleaded with me not to.

Too late – superheated steam filled the shower, as someone gently threaded a white-hot darning needle ever deeper into the by now terrified Monty, heading in the direction of Messi and Ronaldo, my faithful goolies.

This was my introduction to Thai food – Monty and I were not impressed.

I resolved to be on the first plane back to Tenerife if I had to spend one more second of my life eating what the Thais eat.

I had seen enough white faces on the bus as it had entered

Pattaya; surely there had to be some real food somewhere in the city.

CHAPTER 3
FLASHBACK

For the rest of the day, I stayed in my hotel room unable to venture more than a few yards from the toilet and unable to even think about going to see Lek.

Monty was up for it, as were Messi and Ronaldo, but my aris on numerous occasions reminded me that it would be better to stay in and watch the telly.

Day 2 was equally bad and nothing that I ate stayed in my body for more than a few seconds.

I was becoming dehydrated and delirious; my mind entered into its time machine, back to a time when I had suffered a similar bout of volcanic aris syndrome thanks to a dog shit flavoured cocktail of toxicity served up by an equally inscrutable and sadistic Oriental in Malaya.

My head was spinning.

I was hallucinating.

I could hear a screeching sound, a painful torturous sound, something was in great pain, agony almost, and flashing before my eyes was a strange man wearing a skirt and a funny hat.

I had moved back in time, and gradually the visions became clearer.

A couple of very strange people had greeted me on my arrival at Changi airport in Singapore.

As I was straight out of training camp and had barely ventured farther than the outskirts of my hometown mining village; to be confronted by a genetically modified offshoot of Homo Sapiens that had evolved in complete isolation in a village called Glasgow, deep in the ancient English colony of Scotland, was quite a cultural shock.

An alien species

At Grammar school, I had become quite proficient in both French and German, but any form of communication in Glaswegian was impossible and was usually conducted in sign language with the help of 2 fingers.

I have recounted some of my earlier experiences in my book Fishing and Testicles, particularly my constant problems with the cretinous Sgt McTavish, so I will move on a few months.

Out of the blue, a vacancy arose at the main pay office in Sembawang, and not wishing to spend the next 3 years in total intellectual isolation among the skirt wearing tribe of missing link Neanderthals, I took my chance and once again found myself able to communicate with the people around me without having to end each sentence with the word Jimmy or to be awakened every morning by the screeching sound of Sgt McTavish strangling a cat, colloquially known as a bagpipe.

After a couple of months, a chap called Ginger appeared and was stuck in the same room as Flip, Boz and me. Now Ginger wasn't particularly bright, he was, however, a keen fisherman and a few days later found him sat at the next swim to me on one of the army matches held at Lim's pool.

Not particularly bright was Ginger

After 6 hours of fishing, during which time a dozen or more empty cans of Tiger beer were strewn behind the pair of us, and a near 100 pounds of carp swam around in my keepnet, Ginger was barely able to stand.

He was no longer lily-white, nor was he pink. Six hours of sitting in the equatorial sun dressed only in a pair of shorts had turned Ginger well beyond the colour ginger; he was now a pulsating fluorescent red, and for the next 2 weeks he lay in a military hospital bed having blisters bigger than dinner plates dressed.

Is that you
Ginger?

Eventually, he was released and resumed his match fishing, this time covered from head to toe in full-body clothing, where he bore a striking resemblance to a Muslim woman dressed in her alluring cotton bin liner.

Flip, Boz, Ginger and I were now quite busy making inroads into the decent number of army and air force girls that were on the base, when one evening Ginger burst into the room, excitedly proclaiming that the following week his wife was arriving from the UK and he had been allocated an apartment in the married quarters.

During the week Ginger sorted out and equipped the apartment and the great day finally arrived.

Now the army isn't always user friendly, and poor Ginger found himself on guard duty the evening that his wife arrived, and so she was picked up at the airport and dropped off at the apartment that Ginger had so lovingly prepared for her.

It was perhaps an hour or so after Ginger's wife entered the apartment that the phone rang in the guard room.

On the other end of the phone was Mrs Ginger, who seemed quite concerned as she calmly explained that there was a lizard in her apartment and that it had been watching her as she took a shower.

The guard commander burst out laughing and explained that every apartment in Singapore had dozens of lizards (geckos) in them and that they kept the mosquitoes and ants down by eating them, he then put the phone down.

Ten minutes later, the phone rang again with the same message, only this time Mrs Ginger was sobbing as she explained that the lizard was now on top of the fridge and would not let her in the kitchen.

Once again, the guard commander laughed as he reassured her that they were quite harmless and every apartment had dozens of them, even in the bedroom, and she would soon get used to them.

On the third ring, Mrs Ginger was by now screaming hysterically and wanted to go home to her mother back in England, so the guard commander rang the duty security man who just happened to be Ginger.

Ten minutes later, Ginger arrived at the apartment only to find his wife sat outside on the steps, crying, and screaming hysterically that she was going to divorce him and wanted to go home to her mum that very night and never wanted to see him again.

I hate you
Ginger

Ginger tried to console her before going into the apartment with his army issue pickaxe handle and Alsatian guard dog.

Within seconds, there was a yell, followed by a scream and the sound of breaking glass as the apartment door burst open.

Out flew the Alsatian, yelping in fear as it disappeared up the road.

Out flew Ginger, running and squealing like a stuck pig with a red-hot poker up its aris.

And out flew an enormous, 8-foot-long monitor lizard, pursuing both a screaming Ginger and a yelping Alsatian up the road.

Every apartment has dozens of them, even in the bedroom

I have often thought about Ginger's wife on being told that she had to share her tiny apartment with over a dozen giant monitor lizards.

Women can be so fickle.

CHAPTER 4
WRONG LEK

It was now the third day of my Thailand sojourn and I finally felt well enough to leave the room without the fear of an unfortunate accident.

My aris still occasionally twitched like a rabbit's nose, but Monty had become restless and insisted that he needed some fresh air.

I needed food.

I hadn't had a bite to eat since leaving Thailand's equivalent of the Savoy Grill and was desperate for anything remotely edible, with the definite exception of Thai food. I had been warned about the laxative qualities of the stuff by a fellow passenger on the flight out, but nothing could have prepared me for the past 2 days, in fact, I was unsure if my internal organs were still inside my body.

I left the hotel, crossed the 500-baht road, and immediately the young girl from the cafe came out shouting "Hello Gary"; she then grabbed my hand and tried to take me inside with her.

There was no way on earth that I would ever be eating there again, but her body language suggested that it wasn't the cuisine that she was tempting me with.

I made my excuses as best I could in Thai-glish and moved on, hopefully in the direction of Lek's bar, the first stop though had to be a pharmacy; I needed Vaseline, and hummed Johnny Cash's "Burning Ring of Fire," which seemed more than appropriate.

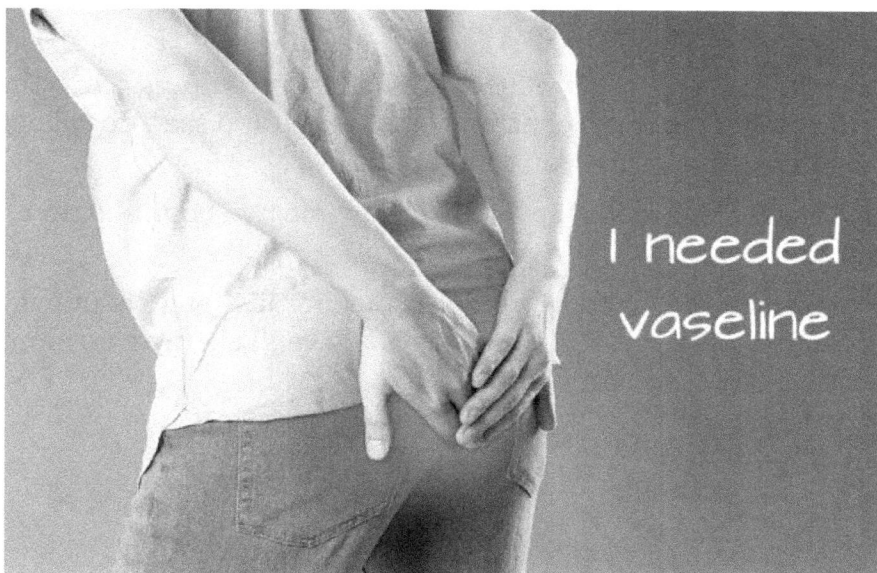

I needed vaseline

Equipped with the lifesaving ointment, I couldn't really apply it in the middle of a busy street, so I popped into a bar and ordered a bottle of Tiger before disappearing into the gents.

On my return, now smiling like a Cheshire cat at the instant relief I had just felt, I found that an overly plump bargirl had deposited herself on the seat next to my beer.

"Hello handsome man," she said. "I'm Lek, who are you?"

This definitely wasn't the Lek that Monty wanted to become more acquainted with, in fact, I doubt that anyone would ever survive the encounter. Her fat aris hung over both sides of the barstool and I imagined myself in a race with her to the nearest pie shop – a race that I dare not lose.

She probably owned her own pie shop.

I temporarily visualised a giant pie disappearing down her throat in one gulp, almost blurting out "You greedy bitch", and just managing to stop myself.

"My name's Garry, Garry Glitter," I said, before gulping down the bottle of Tiger in one, I continued. "Got to go and see a dog about a man now, so bye, see you tonight Lek."

"Bye Garry," she said. "Love you long time, we boom-boom all night."

Ileft the bar in a hurry; I needed a pie, not just any pie but the biggest pie ever baked, a pie so big that even Lek, my enormous newfound love couldn't eat it.

Definitely not the right Lek for Monty

CHAPTER 5
CHEERS

I walked on towards the main tourist area of Pattaya, and as it was becoming dark, I decided to leave Lek's bar for another day and make my way to Little Susy bar in Soi Diane, where I had been assured that Brian, the landlord was expecting me and would point me in the right direction regarding the contacts for a friendly golfing society that he often played with.

Monty tried to go in the opposite direction convinced that Lek would still be waiting for us, but before a raging argument could break out a motorbike equipped with a sort of glass covered side-car pulled up alongside me displaying the sign SIRINAN PIES, I kid you not.

Manna from heaven

This was a lifesaver, there was nothing else in the entire world that I craved more than a pie.

Now you may wonder about my obsession with pies.

Well, I was brought up close to the mill and mining town of

Wigan in Lancashire, and Wigan is without question the pie capital of the world; a Wigan mixed grill being 2 different pies with a pasty, and a Wigan vegetarian meal being a meat and potato pie with the meat taken out.

I bought and gulped down 2 in quick time, regretting that I hadn't bought the third one, before continuing down the Soi (street).

Wigan restaurant at lunch time

PIE EATING CONTEST?

NAH SON. FREE PIE.

Little Susy bar is only a small place with seating for barely a dozen customers and was full of ex-pats, two of whom I knew from my fishing days many, many years earlier.

Several noggins of Tiger beer later I raised my glass and said "Cheers".

"As you are in Thailand Bill," one of the ex-pats said. "You should say 'Chag Well', that is the Thai equivalent of cheers."

Now I have no idea how Chag Well is spelt but I took it on board and for the next 2 weeks, whenever I had a drink with anyone I always politely said Chag Well.

Chag well everyone

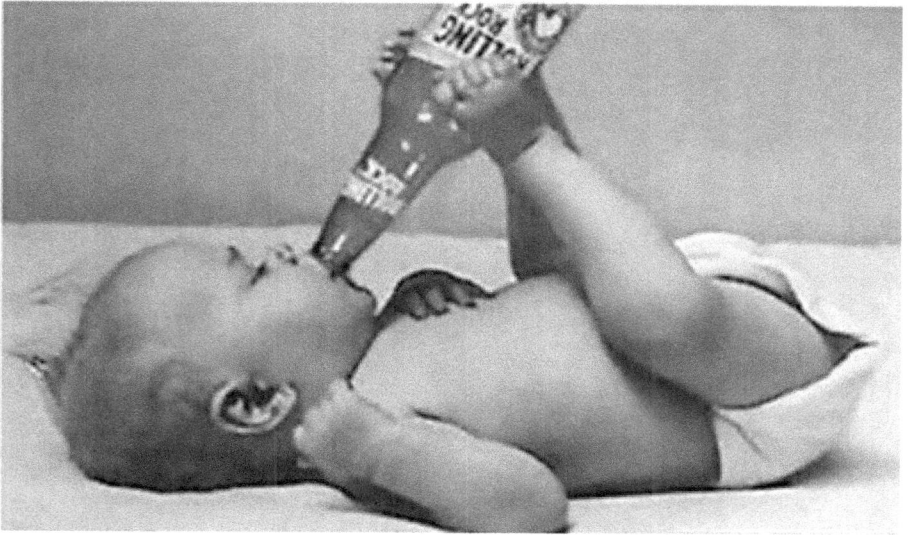

It was a couple of weeks later that Brian leaned over the bar, and with a big grin on his face told me that Chag Well did not in fact mean Cheers but meant WANKER, and so for the past 2 weeks I had been calling everyone I met "Wanker".

I wondered why people had been shunning me.

Why always me?

Do I look that dumb?

Back to the first night at Little Susy bar.

One thing that caught my eye as I was sat at the bar was the number of gorgeous, semi-clad young ladies that were walking up and down the road, many of them supporting men that were too old to even walk without assistance.

My first thought was perhaps the proximity of either a crematorium, where they would be waiting their turn to be burned, this way cutting out   the middleman, or perhaps even a geriatric home, if so, it must have been one hell of a size as the procession was non-stop.

Just popping over to the crematorium dear

Volunteer

One particularly gorgeous young lady aged perhaps around 20 who had been stood on the road alongside the bar noticed that I had become quite fixated with her legs, Monty also paying attention to them.

She walked over to me with a big smile on her face, kissed me and gently patted Monty, who immediately stopped sulking over not going to Lek's bar.

It was pretty obvious that she recognised me from some old photograph of my fishing days and would shortly be asking for my autograph.

Instead, she asked me for 1,000 baht.

I was confused.

She then grabbed me, pulled me tight against her body, and began to give me the simulated Thai version of a jolly good rogering, fully clothed, and at the same time between thrusts gasping "1,000 Baht – er – er – short time – er – er – 1,000 baht."

My mind exploded - Monty gasped

Without going into too much detail, I almost had the short time while still stood at the bar.

It was a most enlightening experience, totally unexpected, nevertheless not too unpleasant.

Monty was absolutely livid when I informed him that we were going back to the hotel a couple of hours later – alone.

He clung desperately to the bar stool

I had to explain to him that I wasn't 100% sure that my aris could be relied on to behave itself before he would release his grip.

There was still some lingering, residual malevolence from the Thai meal deep inside my body just waiting to attack at the first sign of weakness.

Many people who come to Thailand learn this lesson the hard way.

CHAPTER 6
IRENA

I suppose that I had been staying at the Diana Inn for a week or so before I discovered that the hotel laid on a complimentary bus to take people into the tourist area of town every 2 hours, returning on the hour in between, so I began to use this service every evening.

For 4 days there had been a rather dishy white girl called Irena on the late bus returning to the hotel who told me that she was 24 and came from Kyiv in Ukraine.

Accompanying Irena on a couple of occasions was a petite Thai girl of around 16 called Duane, who smiled beautifully whenever I looked at her – Monty overcame his natural shyness and waved an acknowledgement on each occasion.

Now being in Thailand and becoming slightly more streetwise, it was fairly obvious to me that Irena was of the species known as Homo Lesbeus as opposed to Homo Erectus and would during the course of the evening be performing certain gymnastics with her little Thai girl that could possibly raise the dead if accompanied by enough volume.

Monty was curious, and later that evening as we left the bus, I had to explain the differences between the 2 species.

I moved into fantasy mode and once again entered my time machine, this time without the delusional effects of the Thai meal and dehydration.

Growing up in a Lancashire coal mining village, there were no such problems and there was nothing to explain, only two gen-

ders ever existed.

Hello
honkytonk

Life was so simple in those innocent days – men were men and ruled the roost and women stayed in their natural habitat and cooked the meals as nature had always intended.

I suppose that I was in my early teens when I first heard about the evolution of an alien species known as a Poof.

Fortunately, this scary creature was confined to the southerly most parts of England, in particular around London, and was unlikely to ever venture north of Watford Gap.

A couple of years later, at the time when our teenage hormones were beginning to run riot, a fourth species emerged. Now this one was much more interesting and was known as a Lezzie.

From the limited amount of information that was available to fuel our teenage fantasies at the time, we were assured that these Lezzies had been assembled in exactly the same way as women, and when together they performed a series of never-ending sexual perversions without the need for a man being present.

We became very interested, as by studying the drawings on the school toilet walls, we had become graphically aware of what the birds and bees did to each other, yet the question of what Lezzies actually did to fellow Lezzies was still very much a mystery.

What an appalling waste

I can vaguely remember asking our school form master about Poofs and Lezzies, only to discover that he knew even less than we did, emphasising that it was a Southern thing and was never really going to affect us in Lancashire.

It was quite a few years later during an odd drink or two in a Malayan bar with a few army friends that I became aware of a 5th species.

I have described the experience in my book Fishing and Testicles, suffice to say that this particular example of the species was called Norma, and after two hours of emotional and financial expenditure Norma turned out to be Norman.

Oh Norma - stunning but slightly flawed

Now, believe it or not, nothing about sex was ever discussed in either the home or at school, and whatever knowledge we acquired was because of whispered schoolboy rumours.

Thinking myself pretty worldly-wise, my arrival in Pattaya was to prove quite a cultural shock to the system.

Evolution had run amok.

The 5 species that I had previously encountered were the tip of the iceberg – the list was mind-blowing and reminiscent of the old football pools; the male and female of the species had morphed into an endless variety of permutations.

Norma had been a Ladyboy – Pattaya had thousands of them, some with the crown jewels still attached and some, where major structural engineering work had been carried out on the lower sections of the anatomy. As the sense of adventure of most Englishmen extends to no more than a booze-fuelled week in

Benidorm, perhaps I should explain a little more about the lady-boys of Thailand.

In its simplest form, a ladyboy starts out in life as a baby boy and for many years encounters few problems. On reaching puberty a little confusion begins to set in when his eyes spend more time looking at the other boys in his class than at the girls, and dresses occupy most of the space in his wardrobe.

During his late teens, the transition is fairly complete, but unlike gay men, he now considers himself to be a woman trapped inside a man's body.

Hormonal drugs are taken to enhance the boobs and the waist-line shrinks to that of a size zero model. Often, a little surgery is performed around the facial area and silicone implants replace the smaller breasts. The overall package can be quite spectacular. They become very beautiful women as anyone who has encountered the Thai ladyboys will tell you.

My Malayan sweety Norma was a Kai Tai, the Singapore name for a ladyboy, and because of my slightly inebriated state and my total inexperience of the Far East, fooled me completely for a couple of hours.

Norma, however, was not the finished article, as I discovered when my hand wandered a little too close to the bikini line.

No matter how spectacular the boobs and the waistline, there will always be a problem with the Crown Jewels. In order to complete the illusion of total femininity, these things have to be either tucked away and disguised, or they have to be removed completely. I know nothing about the disguising technique, however, the removal technique I imagine could be quite eye-watering, and involves the construction of a false vagina using the scrotum (the testicle receptacle)

Needless to say, both the testicles and their next-door neighbour become history, and as no protein is ever wasted in Thailand, I will leave the rest to your imagination.

Back to the pandora's box of
strange sexual variants.

Prancing around like constipated prima donnas were the usual effeminate Poofs; there were also Harley Davidson riding, leather-clad, rocker Poofs.

The Lezzies of the Western world were somehow different in Pattaya. These scantily clad girls smiled and cavorted with the bar customers; their sexual compliance was both willing and absolute even though their soul mate was a fellow Lezzie.

These soul mates were also completely different to the European Lezzies and were called Tomboys or Toms, often having more muscles than a bodybuilder, and together with their close-cropped hair always dressed in the most masculine clothes imaginable.

A tomboy
cutee

They also took male hormones; their feminine curves being replaced by an almost androgynous gorilla-like shape.

Perhaps the most amazing thing about the "Toms" was that they were always accompanied by a totty with the looks and figure of a film star.

Bar girls often visit Thai clubs to buy (hire) young Thai men for the night, mixing and matching with friends, both male and female, depending on how the mood takes them before returning home to their gorilla Toms.

Their partners don't always look like apes.

There are endless sexual species and subspecies of assumed humans in Pattaya, and like an old Victorian explorer, I am still finding new previously undiscovered gender variations.

I would guess that an archaeologist could unearth innumerable fossilised versions of early sexual variants were he ever to excavate the substrata of Pattaya, and if Charles Darwin had visited the place instead of the Galapagos islands, his masterpiece, The

Origin of Species, may well have gone in a completely different direction, and his timescale of evolution would almost certainly have been greatly accelerated.

Maybe this is one of the main attractions of the place, however, just as in my early schoolboy days, only one species holds any interest to either me or Monty – honest, like all fisherman I never lie.

CHAPTER 7
(Irena 2)

Back to Irena, the Ukrainian beauty and why not?

On the fifth day of returning to the hotel on the complimentary bus, I struck up a conversation with Irena and asked her if she would like to go out for a meal the next evening.

"Sorry Billy," she said in perfect English. "I return to Kyiv tomorrow."

I was crestfallen – rejected again. What did I really expect at my age with a gorgeous 24-year-old?

"Why don't we go now?" she said. "I haven't eaten since this afternoon."

Monty's ears pricked up, completely ignoring the lecture I had given him on Lezzies.

We jumped off the bus, jumped in a taxi and returned to town, where I discovered that like me, she enjoyed Indian food.

We moved on to Little Susy bar and drank into the early hours before once again jumping in a taxi.

As we returned to the hotel I almost passed out when she said, "Your room or mine Billy?"

"What about your Thai girlfriend?" I stammered.

"She isn't a girlfriend," she laughed as she spoke. "I like both men and girls. I only come to Pattaya for the sex."

Monty tried to climb out of my shorts on hearing this. He had always dreamed of a threesome and we had just left 100,000 Thai bargirls back in town. Damn.

"I like both girls and men," said Irena

"Let's have a shower together first," Irena said as we entered her room.

Monty
dragged
me into
the shower

Monty nodded his approval. I in turn viewed the whip on the bed with some suspicion. The black leathers and various other goodies seemed harmless enough, but I do not like pain and I most certainly do not like whips.

Oh Irena –
not the whip

Monty and I waved Irena goodbye the next morning as she set off for the airport.

Monty had found his spiritual home and informed me that if I ever returned to England I would be going alone – he was staying.

Messi and Ronaldo agreed with him.

CHAPTER 8
A LEARNING CURVE

A few weeks into my new life I found myself in a spot of trouble.

The evening had started out innocently enough with a few beers at Little Susy bar in Soi Diana, when Dave, a London taxi driver, asked me if I fancied a walk. Drinking up, we walked on along the road past a few bars until we came to a particular favourite of ours due to the surfeit of totty working there. Here we spied a couple of candy bars gorgeous enough to stop us dead in our tracks.

In we went to be met by two knee-trembling smiles. One was about 20 years old and the slightly taller one around 25.

I grabbed the younger one and left Dave with the old lady.

After a couple of drinks, we both paid the bar fine of 6 quid and headed back to Little Susy bar, the idea being to spend a night on the town with our eye-catching beautiful candy bars.

A bar fine is what you pay the owner of the bar if you want to take one of his girls out for the evening. As he is paying them a salary, it is a form of compensation as they will no longer be working for the rest of the evening. This form of compensation is standard throughout Asia.

Back at the bar, we met up with Kev and Orbi, (my sister's ex-husband) before deciding to take a taxi over to Walking Street.

For people not familiar with Walking Street, it is one of the major at-

tractions in all of Asia and can be described without fear of contradiction as being the sex capital street of the sex capital city of the world times a multiple of 10.

In the 800 yards of its length, if you include the short side streets that branch off it, there are close to 100 Agogo bars plus many normal bars, if indeed you could ever describe a Pattaya bar as being normal.

Walking Street - where ugly
men become filmstars

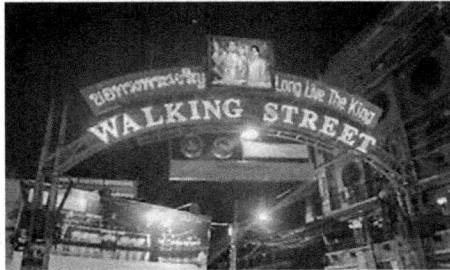

Some of these bars have upwards of 100 girls working in them, and as the whole place is quite expensive, the girls are some of the most beautiful in Asia. Ex-pats rarely go to Walking Street because of the price of everything, leaving the place for the richer Asian and Arab tourists.

However, for a first time Pattaya visitor the place is an absolute must; a heaven on earth sexual paradise where a dead man can be coaxed back to life with little more than a Viagra tablet and a sprinkling of tits and teeth.

Up one of the side streets, passed dozens of semi-naked, beckoning, exquisitely well designed and assembled girls, the 4 of us plus our 2 candy bars trudged and found ourselves in a bar recommended by Dave.

The sight was spectacular, as half a dozen completely naked film stars swivelled and slithered up and down the silver poles; the female hormone scented phallic symbols glistening in the flashing lights.

Scantily clad beauties, both Thai and European, though mostly ex Eastern bloc, lounged around drinking and laughing with customers.

We moved on to the far end of the place and sat around a large square bath with sides around 2 feet high. In the bath were 2 beautiful, totally naked Thai girls who were completely covered in foam and soap bubbles which they were rubbing up and down each other's body.

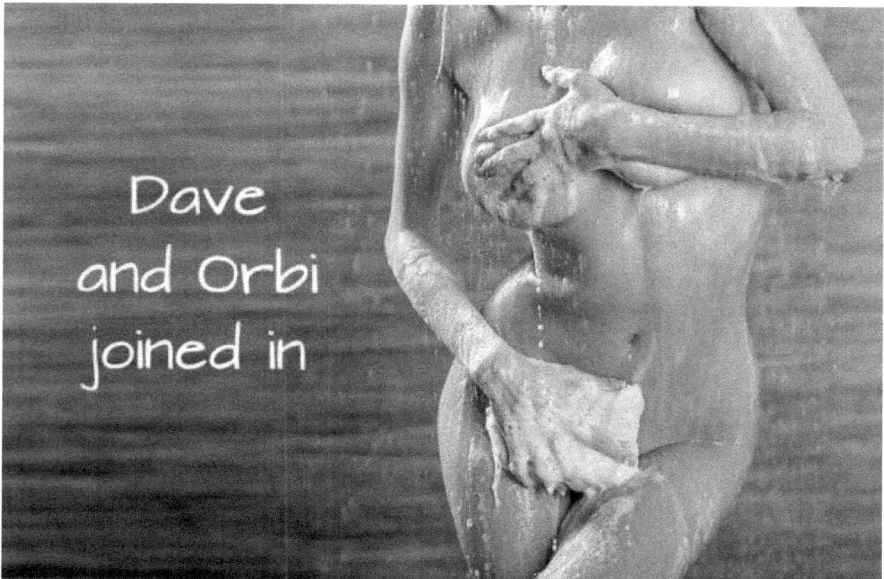

Dave and Orbi joined in

After ordering drinks for the 6 of us, Dave passed over a 100 Baht note (2 quid) to one of the girls who then moved right alongside him. Dave then proceeded to gently massage the girl from head to toe, his hands lingering lovingly around the more sensitive areas. Orbi followed Dave's lead and started work on the other one, a Cheshire cat-like grin splitting his face from ear to ear.

Why oh why didn't my local pub back home in Lancashire pamper its customers this way?

What is wrong with the English breweries?

As this was going on, my eyes became quite preoccupied with events and I didn't notice the silver horizontal bar above my head, nor had I thought twice at Dave and Orbi's insistence on me sitting at this particular spot.

I soon discovered why.

Dave's girl suddenly broke off contact and gently prised his hand out of somewhere unspeakable beneath the bubbles and foam.

Dave checked that his watch was still on his wrist.

She then moved over to me, fastened both hands on the horizontal pole above my head, and swinging forward Tarzan like, wrapped both of her legs around my neck, at the same time pulling my head forward, my nose disappearing deep into her soapy, fish flavoured equatorial rain forest.

Like being buried in a giant fishy creamcake with flaps

She was not a shaver and appeared to be quite proud of her luxuriant growth as she wiggled and imprisoned me ever tighter, her wing mirrors flapping against my cheeks.

I could barely breathe.

Every time I breathed in there was a loud gasping, gurgling sound and my mouth filled with foam and soap bubbles. Every time I breathed out it sounded as if I was in the middle of a farting competition, her flaps vibrating like violin strings against my cheeks with clouds of bubbles floating off towards the ceiling.

Fishy bubbles floated across the bar

The other members of our party, including the 2 girls, were help-less with laughter and I was powerless to do anything about it, trapped in my own life-threatening fishy hell hole.

Eventually, she released her headlock on me, whereupon I began coughing and spluttering, at the same time spitting out a mix-ture of soap bubbles and wispy bits of her luxuriant Thai jungle.

I wasn't too amused; mind you, everyone else was.

Not for the first time in my life had I become the centre of attrac-tion due to my naivety.

I have temporarily moved on a few months.No more than 200 yards from the beginning of Walking Street is the Sugar Shack, the bar that hosts the golf society that I became a member of.

One evening, after a few drinks in the bar, Lek, (a later addition to Monty's carefully selected collection of all-time favourites and the girl on the bus from the airport) and I walked the 50 or so yards to a bar sporting a sign that said, "Cabaret every night".

Lek shook her head and informed me that it wasn't a good idea to go in. Monty tried to go in the opposite direction, nevertheless, ignoring both Monty and Lek's protests, I grabbed Lek's hand and dragged her inside.

The place was full of men without a lady in sight.

Monty shrunk and refused to look at proceedings.

I soon discovered why.

On to the stage strode half a dozen young men in their early twenties. They then proceeded to seductively undress each other in time to the music, kissing and performing a different version of cabaret to the one that I was expecting.

An unexpected cabaret

Lek protectively placed her hand over Monty's eye, not wishing him to see what was going on – the pair of them had been getting on rather well for the past few months and were rarely parted.

We didn't stay long in that bar, a couple of minutes at the most, and on reaching fresh air a grinning Lek said, "I did try to warn you, but not only are you stubborn, sometimes you can be pretty stupid." She then pointed her finger skyward, and above our heads was a massive sign that crossed from one side of the road to the other, saying in giant letters – BOYS TOWN.

The entire area was full of cabaret and Agogo bars, none of which contained one single female.

"We did warn you," said Lek and Monty

I couldn't wait to leave BOYS TOWN and return to the part of town where men are still men, and a Thai bar girl's job is to facilitate the redistribution of wealth from the Western world to some remote village deep in the Thai jungle hinterland.

Perhaps you can now understand that even though I can try to describe Pattaya, you will never fully understand what the place is about until you have actually been here.

Living in the affluent Western World it would be easy yet very wrong to be too judgmental at the lifestyle over here. When rats, fried bugs, and various creatures form a staple part of the villager's diet, a different culture and an equally different form of morality has developed over many generations often out of necessity.

Vive la Difference.

CHAPTER 9
DUANE

I had managed a few noggins at Little Susy bar one evening when Bob said that he fancied a walk-in search of fresh totty and knew of a bar down Soi Buakhao where a particular favourite bar girl of his plied her trade.

"She's deaf and dumb," he said. "But she makes up for it in every other way."

"Sounds good to me," I replied. "Has she got a sister who can't speak?"

Halfway to the bar in question, I got accosted by an exquisite display of tits and teeth and simply had to go inside the bar with her.

Bob carried on in search of his ideal woman.

I bought my bronze, dark-haired beauty a drink and sat down next to her at the bar where the usual pleasantries were exchanged, and quite out of the blue, she reached out and introduced herself to Monty by gently shaking him.

Now in England, it is quite common to shake hands with someone that you meet for the first time; however, I am quite convinced that the Thai way is infinitely superior and should be adopted as a world standard.

Monty immediately fell in love and refused to let go of her hand, which lingered for several seconds before she finally reached for her drink.

I have to say that of the multitude of women we had seen so far, I was well impressed with Monty's choice and told him so.

Already standing to attention, he saluted.

Well into our 4th drink, the girl suddenly jumped up and said. "Got to go now, my boyfriend he just come in."

Sure enough, across the room came a rather large figure who put his arm around the girl and glared at me.

Monty was up for the fight, I, however, noted that not only did he look like an ape, but he was also built like one.

I smiled inwardly as a mental picture of David Attenborough feeding him a banana flashed through my subconscious. I had seen that image many times in my nightmares – could the ape possibly be Sgt McTavish, the bagpipe playing Glaswegian retard from my army days?

It was time to move on and find Bob, having learned the first and most important rule of Pattaya.

YOU NEVER LOSE YOUR GIRL IN PATTAYA
- ONLY YOUR TURN.

I paid for the beer that I had drunk, plus the 4 lady-drinks, and moved on along Soi Buakhao heading towards the bar that Bob was in, probably sitting in total silence with his deaf and dumb girl, when my eyes fixed on a rather pretty little darling sporting wonderful tits and teeth that was walking towards me.

She looked familiar, and as she got closer, I recognised her as the little lezzie totty that had been sat on the bus with Irena.

"Hello Billy," she said, her low-cut skimpy dress revealing two perfectly developed boobs for such a young girl.

"Hello," I replied. "Where are you off to?"

Duane was off to work as an Agogo dancer in Kiss bar, Soi Metro, and despite looking barely 16 she was in fact 26.

Duane
warming up
for work

Even more importantly, Duane was most certainly no lezzie.

Duane bordered nymphomania and moved in with me 3 days later, whereupon Monty set out to immerse and indulge himself in her wonderful, medical affliction.

Tenerife was becoming a distant memory – another world, a clean, sanitised, organised world.

This world was disorganised, manic, self-indulgent, and hedonistic.

This world was my kind of world.

Mine and Monty's.

CHAPTER 10
DUANE (2)

Duane and Monty hit it off together from day one and were rarely apart.

There were times when I felt completely out of place and began to develop the "three's a crowd" syndrome.

Duane was insatiable, and often I would awake at 3 in the morning to find that both her and Monty had been playing together for over an hour without even bothering to wake me.

I was becoming jealous of Monty's success – I was paying for everything yet he was having all the fun.

Come on Monty

After a few months, Duane was becoming homesick and wanted to visit her family back in a jungle village just across the border in Laos, so we flew up to Udon Thani and took a taxi the 50 or so miles to the village.

The contrast between the bright lights and chaotic vibrance of Pattaya and the third world snail-like momentum of the jungle village was immense.

Even though we were now in Laos, no-one seemed to do anything other than to indulge in the Thai National sport of screwing each other at every possible opportunity – there were kids everywhere. It was as if I had been transported into the African jungle and had joined up with a troop of Colobus monkeys.

It was also noticeable that everyone looked pretty much the same, an androgynous slightly mutated variation of a form of homo sapiens, all wearing pretty much the same face mask.

Now I have previously mentioned the unusual combination of sexual variants to be found in Pattaya, well, pretty much most of them can be found in one single family in these remote Southern Laotian villages.

Duane's father bore more than a passing resemblance to a baboon, this feature running through the entire family, in fact most of the village.

I looked closely at Duane and could see no possible link, leaving the question of her lineage open to conjecture.

Had I discovered the missing link in this remote Laotian jungle village?

Was this the Oriental version of Piltdown man?

Was it something in the water I wondered?

Her younger brother was a poof who was married to a girl that lived with her current boyfriend 2 houses away. She had 3 identical baboon featured children fathered by a different man who was living in a house between their 2 houses.

Confused? It gets worse.

Her older brother was a ladyboy living and working in the tourist sector of Chang Mai, and both of her twin sisters were lesbians, one of which was a knuckle-dragging Tom who would have scared Mike Tyson shitless.

That only left Duane and Boah.

As you have probably guessed, Duane was a nymphomaniac bisexual, and Boah was an eating machine married to an enormous German called Hans.

In the wooden shack that all the family seemed to live in, was a small black and white television and one single fan. I was thankful that I had booked into the Udon Thani hotel for a few nights

Home
sweet
home

The only redeeming feature of the jungle village was the village shop, some 50% of which was devoted to beer – it soon became clear why.

In between bouts of screwing anything with a pulse, the villagers drink, and if they have enough money they don't stop drinking until either the money runs out or they pass out.

It was after some eleventeen bottles of Leo beer that I called the taxi to take Duane and I back to our Udon Thani hotel, at the same time as her woofter brother left the garden with an armful of snares.

What the hell was he up to? As far as I knew there were few rabbits in Laos.

The next morning I was to pick up a hire car, and together with Boah and Hans, we were back off to Laos to visit the ancient French-influenced capital city of Vientiane alongside the mighty Mekong River.

Bright and early I picked up the hire car and drove across the border to the village of the baboon troop just in time to see Duane's woofter brother emerge from the undergrowth complete with an arm full of snares and carrying a sack that was bouncing in all directions. Inside the sack were some 50 or so rats, snared during the night in the sugar cane fields alongside the village. Duane informed me that these rodents were to be the breakfast for the entire village, and when barbecued tasted exactly like chicken.

I drove on into Vientiane, where true to form, Boah sought out the nearest restaurant, not having eaten for a couple of hours.

The open-air restaurant seemed clean enough, so the 2 girls ordered a selection of dishes that someone else had eaten the previous day and brought back up, while Hans and I settled for a sandwich each.

The dish with the chicken feet looked particularly delicious

Duane spoke to the waiter in what appeared to be a chimpanzee dialect and he disappeared, returning a minute later with a bowl of red-hot chillies.

Painful to even look at

I glared at Duane.

Hans glared at Boah.

It had been a couple of months earlier after Duane had finished a late meal with a bowl of red-hot chilli, that she grabbed Monty and dragged him into the bedroom for a spot of exercise.

Fancying something a little different, Duane had disappeared under the bedclothes.

Perhaps 30 seconds had elapsed before Monty suddenly let out an agonising scream and dragged me into the bathroom before submersing himself in a glass of cold water from which he refused to emerge for over half an hour.

Hans and I were obviously on the same wavelength, something that he later confirmed on the journey home.

Poor Hans
- no more
chilli
before
bed Boah

It was towards the end of the meal that the commotion began. Someone had set the chip fryer on fire and a small wisp of smoke started to waft out of the kitchen.

Duane saw it first and at the top of her voice shouted FIRE! On hearing this, a general panic set in, and some 50 people stood up and ran, knocking the tables, meals, and drinks everywhere.

The poor owner of the restaurant tried to stop the mad exodus but got trampled in the stampede, losing the money from 50 meals and drinks.

Hans and I carried on drinking as the 2 girls ran off down the road like headless chickens, carried along by the herd mentality.

Hans and I were the only ones to pay the bill.

We left the heart-broken and considerably poorer owner and walked on in the direction that the stampede had followed, eventually finding the girls naturally enough eating again, Boah having persuaded Duane to go into yet another restaurant for even more regurgitated slop.

After Boah had finished her second plate of dung we set off to explore the city.

Now for the people who have never visited the Far East, there is a wonderful tree that has fibrous roots that hang from the middle branches right down to the ground. Walking under such a tree, I couldn't resist tugging at the hanging roots.

Whups, and down came the Banyan tree branch

The tug dislodged a loose branch which promptly fell and landed on two suited and booted Chinese businessmen that were walking behind us.

We walked on as one dazed and bemused chap picked himself up and rubbed his head wondering what the hell had just hit him, and the other one stayed down moaning, a drop or two of blood running down his face.

Whups

There was to be more fun and games to come later.

We settled into an open bar alongside the Mekong river and began to make inroads into the Laotian beer, in Boah's case accompanied by a succession of different meals. Her food intake was enormous, and not wishing to be on the menu I ensured that the hotel room door was securely locked later that evening.

It was some eleventeen bottles later and I was feeling a little dizzy.

The beautiful Mekong river mesmerizingly meandered by the restaurant as it wove its hypnotic spell.

My mind began to wander, and I entered my time machine and transported myself back to my Far East army days.

Days of wonder and days of menace.

CHAPTER 11
BILLY BILKO

Having wangled a posting away from the Neanderthal occupied Jock city of Nee Soon with its caterwauling morning bagpipe reveille, I took up my new position at Sembawang, where I was put in charge of foreign currency transactions.

Strangling a cat

Now anyone knowing me will almost certainly see that the army had made a big mistake.

There can only be one outcome if you put a fox in charge of the chicken coup.

I spent the first week being taught the job by Colin M, whose parting shot was. "I'm off to England tomorrow Billy and I am going to retire. You are now the only one on the island who has a clue what you are doing." He then smiled, winked, and walked away without saying another word.

Colin was right, I was now the king of the castle, and if he could retire in his mid-twenties, what could a cunning genius mind like mine achieve?

It took me little more than a couple of days to crack and bi-pass the system that the army had spent a couple of centuries perfecting.

Without going into too much detail, there were two types of money. One was the fixed-forces rate which the soldiers were paid at, and one was the local bank rate, the difference being some 15%.

The army had now put the lunatic in charge of the asylum, and with over a dozen foreign currencies to work with and no one having a clue of what I was up to, the possibilities were endless.

It would have been selfish of me to keep everything for myself, so Flip, Boz, and Mike, their boss in charge of the transport pool, were included in most of my money-making schemes.

I have to point out that nothing illegal took place, however, the word unethical springs to mind.

As Ginger had moved on to live with his wife and their dozen pet monitor lizards, Ray moved into our room. Now Ray was in charge of the mess (dining arrangements), and would obviously prove useful in the near future, so I included him in my select little group. The wisdom of such a move soon became apparent as I became the only soldier in the entire British Empire who had his own personal menu, with his dinner cooked individually by a qualified chef and then delivered to the office.

No army
food
for me

Ray in turn began to accumulate wealth faster than the Brigadier, as did all of my little circle of useful friends.

My direct boss, Major M, looked on quite aware that I was up to something as rumours were beginning to circulate of my group dining out at the Shangri-La hotel a couple of times a week, something that even he couldn't afford on a Major's salary. Eventually, he cracked and asked to be included in the group. This was now the perfect set up, (possibly the perfect storm) as Major M was the man who signed off on all my "business" transactions, and he in turn became only the second soldier in the entire British Empire to have his own personal chef.

The rest of the office looked on enviously as Major M and I tucked into Ray's culinary creations, while they had to go to the mess and eat standard army grub.

Knowing my connections with the transport lads, and now being included in my inner circle, one day, Major M asked if I could possibly arrange for a Land Rover to pick him up at the office as he had to get home in a hurry to take his wife shopping in the city.

I phoned Mike in the transport pool and 5 minutes later the Brigadier's limo turned up, and from then on, Major M became the only soldier in the entire British Empire below the rank of

Brigadier to have a chauffeur-driven limo take him and his wife shopping every week.

I in turn became the only soldier in the entire British Empire that went fishing every afternoon, delivered, and returned by a chauffeur-driven Land Rover, the chauffeur being either Flip or Boz and the packed lunch being supplied by Ray.

God, I was missing England – Sergeant Bilko had nothing on me, and in the Transport pool, my nickname soon became Billy Bilko, as travel expense claims and overnight stay funding rapidly depleted the MOD's allocation of taxpayer's money.

The original Sgt. Bilko

One day, 3 newly posted and extremely pretty, young WRAC's appeared in the office, and although this wasn't really my area of responsibility, I was up like a shot with the necessary forms. That evening, together with Flip and Boz, we found ourselves entertaining them in a local bar, where after a little discussion between the 3 of us, we made the necessary selection.

I chose the smaller of the three who just happened to have enormous boobs and a beautiful smile.

I have always been a sucker for tits and teeth.

Monty could never resist a beautiful smile

After working on them for a week or so, I walked into Major M's office one afternoon just before his limo was due to arrive for his weekly shopping trip, with a form for him to sign.

He viewed it suspiciously, as on the top of the form it read "Army Adventure Training Scheme".

Now the form was genuine enough, and the idea was for a group of soldiers to go out in the field and to do a study with some sort of military significance attached, all paid for by the army.

The scheme that I had concocted was to travel up the East coast of Malaya and to chart the invasion route that the Japanese had taken during the second world war on their way to capturing Singapore.

Absolutely unmitigated genius looking back on it.

"The form says 6 people", Major M said. "I take it that means you, Boz and Flip, so who are the other 3?" He paused for a few seconds before going on. "They wouldn't by any chance be those recently arrived WRAC's that I saw you talking to in the office last week, would they?"

"Well actually sir, I was kind of hoping that you would make a phone call to the WRAC captain and sort it for me, and then sign the form before your transport arrives, your wife will be waiting for you, sir."

A few days later, the long-wheelbase Land Rover crossed the causeway from Singapore to Malaya complete with camping gear and 6 passengers, as it made its way up the East Coast on its way to Terengganu for a spot of adventure training; not necessarily the type of adventure training that the army had visualised.

We carefully avoided the route that the invading Japanese army had taken during the second world war, as some of the sneaky bastards might have still been hiding in the undergrowth.

The first evening we didn't even unload and having found a friendly bar by the beach, we drunk ourselves into oblivion before crashing out on the beach under a beautiful tropical moon having put the adventure training on hold.

Ready for orders Bilko

We spent the next day drinking, eating, swimming with giant turtles, and snorkelling, before building a whacking great bonfire and settling down for copious amounts of adventure training, fuelled and lubricated by a few dozen cans of Tiger beer and a couple of bottles of Bacardi.

The girls were now loosening up, and the six of us completely stripped for an evening's swim before pairing up by our campfire wrapped only in a towel each.

It was now time for some serious adventure training, and things were really hotting up when suddenly one of the girls let out a terrified scream. "It's a Dragon."

Monty stopped whatever he was doing and had a good look round.

A real live dragon was heading our way

We all jumped up, and running towards us in the full light of the moon was a bloody great monitor lizard, snarling and spitting.

There was no-where to run and escape on the open beach, so we began running around the campfire chased by this psychopathic creature who probably had some buried eggs nearby.

Tits and teeth in full flight

At this point, you must use your imagination.

The towels had all dropped off, and 3 screaming girls ran for their lives around the bonfire, 2 of them peeing themselves and their tits flying in every direction, followed by three young soldiers all sporting a hard on.

It was at this point that I discovered that it is impossible to run with a hard on, so one hand must steady the ship and take a firm grip.

Equally, a woman cannot run with her tits out, as they both fly off in different directions resulting in a complete loss of balance.

At the sight of this, Flip, Boz, and myself collapsed in a heap, laughing uncontrollable, and with our spare hand, resorted to hurling handfuls of sand at the dragon until it eventually got bored and slunk off back into the undergrowth.

There was to be no further adventure training that evening, the momentum was lost, as covered in sand and still laughing hysterically, we again went for a swim before finishing the beer and Bacardi and again passing out on the beach; me dreaming of breaking the ice on the local Leigh canal and catching sod all fish once again.

God, Billy Bilko wasn't half missing the Lancashire coalfields, the horrendous Winter weather and Blake's dark satanic mills.

CHAPTER 12
NELLIE THE ELEPHANT

As the light began to fade, (back to Laos) and multi-coloured images reflected along the mighty Mekong river, my mind returned to the present just in time to see Boah put the finishing touches to yet another meal.

"I'm hungry," said Hans. "Let's go and find a place that does food instead of this Laos crap."

In the short space of time that Hans had been in my company, his English had improved dramatically.

Off we staggered in the direction of the night market, where several dozen tables were laid out and several vendors were selling various dishes of fried insects and creatures.

Yum bloody yum

We were just about to leave when we noticed one that sold fish, which on closer inspection turned out to be Tilapia, a home-grown species that both Hans and I recognised as being edible as it is sold all over Thailand.

Boah chose the biggest one on display, and soon we were all tucking into a very nice cheap meal.

On finishing the fish, washed down with yet another bottle of Laotion beer, the 4 of us decided to explore the market.

I soon got bored of staring at dead rats, cockroach type beetles, various assorted bugs, chicken bottoms, and pigs' penises, so at Monty's insistence, I chose to stand by the road observing the Laotion tits and teeth at closer quarters.

Across the road, a man walked along with an elephant on a chain.

Laotian folk can be very strange and I couldn't help wondering why he didn't get himself a dog as a pet, which would surely be much cheaper to feed. Maybe he had an allotment and used the elephant dung for his rhubarb; then again, perhaps it was an integral part of the country's cuisine; from the smell of the stuff that Boah had been tucking into this was probably the answer.

As he reached directly opposite me, the elephant stopped dead in its tracks and glared menacingly at me, giving me the same sort of look usually offered by drunken Glaswegians before accusing you of looking at them and then hitting you over the head with a bottle.

Not wanting to offend or antagonize the creature, I tried not to catch its eye.

It continued to glare at me, so I smiled.

This didn't work.

Despite the valiant efforts of the 5ft man who was taking it for a walk, the elephant continued to fix me with its evil little piggy eyes before heading across the road directly towards me, picking up speed as it charged.

Oh shit!

Cars screeched to a halt – the man dragged on the chain and beat it with a stick, all to no avail – several tons of bushmeat takes some stopping.

"Clucking Bells," I thought. "I'm dead."

I couldn't move; I was completely immobilised with fear.

Monty was in a state of blind panic and screaming at me to get out of the way.

Suddenly, just as I was about to be either trampled as flat as a well-ironed eunuch's scrotum or have 18 inches of pointed Ivory thrust up my bottom, Hans grabbed me and pulled me out of the way.

There was a terrific crash, and the market stall that had been selling big bunches of bananas directly behind where I had been stood was flattened, and Nelly the Elephant tucked in.

Now what was Nellie looking at?

Together, the little Laotion handler and the Indian stall owner whacked away at the beast with sticks – Nelly simply carried on feeding regardless.

I had just witnessed the only creature in the Far East that could eat more than Boah.

It was time to go and find a hotel, my underwear needed changing and Monty had simply disappeared into thin air along with Messi and Ronaldo.

CHAPTER 13
DUANE (3) AND RATTY

We left the hotel quite early the next morning, arriving at the Baboon palace around mid-day, Duane's first job being to collect the beer and Boah's first task being to cook herself a meal. We had already eaten a full English breakfast at the hotel, Boah had also insisted on stopping shortly after setting out to stock up on food for the 2-hour journey.

Duane's woofter brother had had a good night and everyone in the village had eaten a hearty rat breakfast including the head baboon – Duane's dad, who having eaten his fill, still had one spare 4-legged morsel left over.

This poor rat was rammed into a plastic mesh type of onion bag for the next day's breakfast and left swinging from a tree branch in the near 40-degree heat while the rest of the family downed endless bottles of Leo beer.

This kept me amused for a while, but I began to feel sorry for the poor little rat that was swinging above our heads, so I poured a little beer into a bottle top and held it to the side of the plastic mesh bag. One sniff and he slurped the lot of it, so every time that I poured myself a drink, I topped him up, and without a moment's hesitation, he drank everything that I offered him.

He had seen the fate that had befallen his relatives and quite reasonably wanted to blot out the reality of his own impending doom.

Eventually, it was time to go – I needed food – so I went to give my newfound drinking buddy and soon to be next day's breakfast another sip of beer.

The poor little fella was now lying flat on his back making

strange gurgling and squeaking noises, totally pissed and unable to stand.

Completely
rat arsed

The next morning we returned to the Laos pallet wood version of Chatsworth to be greeted by Duane's dad who was screaming at me in chimpanzee and brandishing a knife.

Sometime during the night the rat had sobered up and chewed his way out of the bag. Duane explained that her dad was convinced that I had returned, released it, and taken it up the pub for a drink.

I, in turn, asked her to explain to him that he would look rather foolish walking around the village with the handle of a kitchen knife protruding out of his bottom.

He put the knife away.

On our return to the Udon Thani hotel, I began to question if it was wise to have a family of multi-sexually orientated baboons as in-laws and a rapacious bi-sexual nymphomaniac as a spouse.

Monty was well up for it but I had my doubt

The next day was to be special, Duane had told me I was in for a treat but I wasn't aware of why.

Unbeknown to me, Duane had told the baboon family that we were engaged to be married, flashing a 2-bob imitation gold ring on her finger to them as proof.

I was now having serious doubts about our relationship.

The very thought of marrying anyone with enough sexual energy to exhaust an entire Welsh male voice choir, **and their wives**, filled me with dread.

Please help doc, I need more men

SEX ADDICTION

I was now a little older than my teenage years, and Monty and

I were beginning to argue over which direction he should be facing, especially while I was still asleep – it wasn't cricket, in fact it was simply damned bad manners to carry on with Duane the way he had been doing without waking me up.

Just 3 more times Monty - please

Another thing that concerned me was the question of whether all Thai and Laotian girls were the same. If so, jumping from the frying pan into the fire seemed pointless.

If the 72 virgins awaiting the Muslim suicide bombers turned out to be Thai Agogo dancers, there would be a rush of trainee Trappist monks.

On reflection, finding 72 oriental virgins would involve checking out 72 prams, as training for the national sport begins very early in life for these girls.

CHAPTER 14
THE ENGAGEMENT FEAST

I drove to the village of the baboon the next morning for what turned out to be an engagement party, with invitations having gone out to most of the family relatives in the village.

This turned out to be quite a surprise, as everyone in the village, both male and female, plus all the various other sexual variants and deviants, did in fact have a hint of baboon about them – something in the water for sure.

I was fated as the guest of honour still unaware of why; they had seen Europeans before; Hans was white and spent a lot of time in the village helping to feed Boah.

After a couple of Leo beers, preparations began for the engagement feast.

The open barbecue was fired up and an enormous great wok heated on a bed of hot coals set up next to it.

Something smelled funny.

Something smelled horribly funny and appeared to be coming from the Barbecue, so I sauntered over to see what was cooking, jumping back in horror at the sight of half a dozen bloody great rats, their fur now on fire. Alongside them in a sort of cage contraption were 20 or so more of their relatives, all still alive, and all waiting for their moment of ritualistic execution and gastronomic glory.

I couldn't help but worry in case one of them had been my drinking partner of the previous day. The baboons and their relatives were eager to begin – this was to be only the first course, worse was to follow.

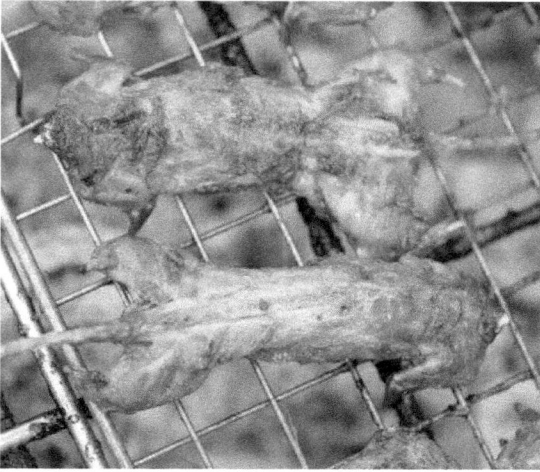

Ratatouille
Thai style

Boah was salivating and Hans held her in a stranglehold.

Into a giant wok went a mix of oil, garlic, and chilli, followed by what appeared to be animal entrails.

Pigs intestines -
a Thai delicacy

The dish was stirred for a couple of minutes, then in went the chicken feet.

Did they throw the rest of the chicken away?

I was beginning to feel queasy.

Hans was now sat on Boah and holding her down.

A large polythene bag was slit open and around 30 giant frogs were emptied into the wok.

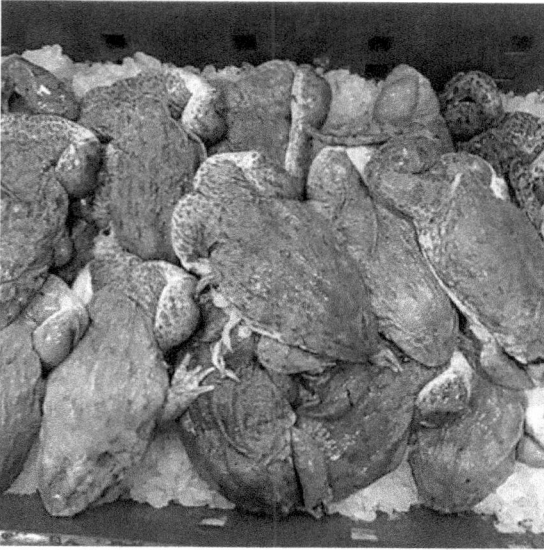

I heaved

Just when I thought that things couldn't get any worse, along came the piece de resistance.

The lid was taken off a pan that was beside the wok and into the mix was tipped a selection of smaller live frogs, cockroach type beetles, scorpions, lizards, and giant caterpillars, all still alive.

On contact with the hot oil, every frog jumped out and set a course for freedom across the garden hotly pursued by an army of hungry baboons.

The family had really pushed the boat out for their young daughter's fiancé, who being a rich Westerner would soon be buying them a new house and car.

Boah was inevitably the first to dine, snatching 2 of the barbecued rats and guarding them like a dog with a bone as she crunched her way through them. The sight of a rat's tail hanging out of her mouth needs no describing.

She then tucked into the bugs.

Legs, wings, body -
Boah ate everything

A few more of the larger grubs and scorpions were threaded on to sticks and placed alongside the rats on the barbecue.

Hans was once again holding Boah down

Every time a plate of creatures appeared in front of me, I passed it under the table to the family dog, who strangely enough also bore a passing resemblance to a baboon.

It is fair to say that if it flies, runs, hops, jumps, swims, crawls, lives in trees, swamps, water, underground, or simply exists in whatever shape or form, the Orientals will lick their lips and eat it.

That evening back in our Udon Thani hotel, Duane snuggled closer to me and pursed her lips in anticipation.

Monty immediately pretended to be fast asleep, I, in turn, visualized the frogs, beetles, scorpions, lizards, and giant caterpillars crawling around inside her, maybe all the way back into her mouth.

It was time to move on - time to seek pastures new.

Somehow the magic had gone.

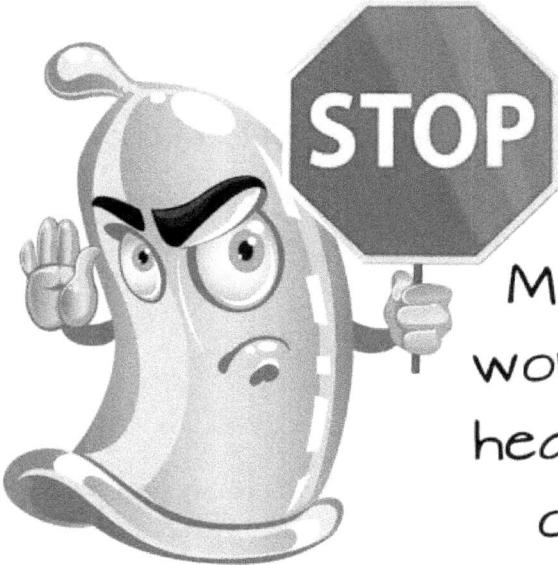

Monty was worn out and heaved a sigh of relief

CHAPTER 15
FREE AT LAST

I had a troubled night's sleep.

Rats were seeking revenge for Boah having eaten half of their colony and were biting my feet, scorpions were poisoning me with their sting, succulent grubs were crawling down my throat and giant frogs were chasing me around the room trying to roger me.

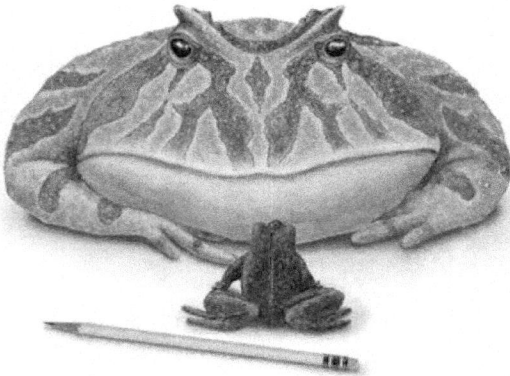

Get off you amphibian pervert

Duane gently climbed on top of me.

Monty pushed her away.

This was to be our last night together – the next day we flew back to Bangkok, and as we took the airport bus to Pattaya I told her so.

She took it calmly enough until we set foot outside of the bus, at which point she attacked, firstly Monty and then me.

You can
stuff the
wedding

A crowd of bemused spectators gathered around, thoroughly enjoying the spectacle and applauding every blow that she landed.

Eventually, she calmed down.

I gave her the money that I had left from our eventful holiday and smiling with the satisfaction she disappeared from my life forever, presumably resuming her erotic dancing around the silver pole at a Pattaya Agogo bar.

Back to
the old job
I guess

I walked forlornly back to my hotel.

Sure enough, out popped my 14-year-old admirer from the Thai Savoy Grill.

"Missed you Gary, where you go?"

"I go to sleep, I tired."

"I come sleep with you Garry; for you free tonight."

I smiled; Monty and I made the 500-baht 20-yard journey to the Diana Inn alone.

I needed a good long sleep and time to think.

Looking back, and having now lived in Pattaya for the last 8 plus years, the place is a little like the Eagles' Hotel California – you can check out, but you can never really leave, and if you meet any man who has holidayed here, he will almost certainly inform you that once you have been to Pattaya, you will forever want to return.

In a nutshell, Pattaya is the sex capital of the world times a multiple of 10.

In comparison, Las Vegas is little more than a Mothercare store.

There are well over 100 Agogo bars and still rising, some 3000 girlie bars and possibly 5000 massage parlours. It is impossible to count the number of girls and young women that work the city – estimates vary from 100,000 right up to quite a lot more.

Already the alarm bell will be ringing as the word prostitution looms large, the very word conjuring up negative images of drugs, violence, pimps, and people trafficking; and so it is throughout the Western world. In certain parts of the Orient, however, there is a completely different perspective on life.

Sex is not only the national sport and a pleasurable pastime, but also a commodity – possibly even a form of currency, and in its wider role, it is in many ways no more than a job that helps to pay the family bills back in the villages.

There are few morality issues involved, and as a comparison, having a coffee with a work colleague in the Western world is often viewed as a far greater sin as rumour and gossip are sure to follow.

"How can you pay for sex?" The puritanical West will ask.

Date a girl in Europe and find out.

By the time you have paid for a meal and a few drinks, you have begun the process of paying for sex, which if my past experiences are anything to go by is anything BUT a foregone conclusion.

The currency may be a little different, but the principle is the same, only in Pattaya, the outcome is guaranteed.

There is also the added bonus that the favour you have just bought will be between 18 and whatever is your upper age limit, extremely beautiful and slim.

Pie eating females have to find different forms of employment in Pattaya.

No pie eaters on the silver pole

She will not moan, complain, nag, nor will she threaten to expose you as a rapist, and in many cases, she will speak very little English other than "Yes

– Yes – Yes as she massages your ego with gusto.

Many of the girls do in fact speak reasonable English, and I have found that discussing the evening's planned entertainment over a meal aids digestion.

CHAPTER 16
SOMETHING DIFFERENT

It was around 2am in the morning as I walked home from an evening's carousing at Little Susy bar that a couple of girls I had got to know (post-Duane) asked me to join them for a drink at a nearby bar.

Despite being a couple of lesbians there would be few raised eyebrows other than excited questions from friends, so I accepted their invitation, walked into the bar with them and bought 3 beers.

Magically, in fact, almost inevitably the conversation turned to sex, a subject discussed as openly among Thai girls as is football among the ex-pats.

The younger of the 2 girls, Gip, was 18, looked 14, and was the "Tomboy" of the two, meaning that she had close-cropped hair and a chest that was as flat as a porridge plate.

She was actually extremely pretty despite dressing as a boy.

I had to ask. "How come your chest is so flat – where are your boobs?"

The reply shocked me, as she reckoned that every morning and night she rubbed special cream onto her boobs and that made them shrink.

"Keep your hands away from my dick," I said.

Monty hid.

She then took off her t-shirt.

The cream's beginning to work

Instead of a bra holding up her boobs, she wore one that flattened them completely.

There was no stirring in the loins from Monty, instead I detected a certain shrinkage coupled with a ring piece that became quite agitated.

Her partner, however, was seriously female; slim, around 25 years old and drop-dead gorgeous.

"I'm Noi," she said. "You like pussy, Billy?"

My mouth flew open in surprise.

Monty's ears pricked up.

She pursed her lips and asked me if I ever had a soapy or an oily massage, I shook my head; her response was quite enlightening.

"Come to Pussy Bar, my massage salon in week," she said. "I give you special oil massage; not tomorrow though, my pussy still sore, I have busy day today."

I took a swig of beer to calm myself down, half of it spilling onto my shirt, and almost immediately Monty made his presence felt.

Monty was all ears and had become quite animated.

Noi then went on to explain her massage technique.

The naked customer lies down on a plastic-covered bed, and she, also completely naked, gently massages perfumed oil into his body with her hands before lying on top of him, and using her body, especially her quite ample boobs, slides up and down in an erotic massage come embrace.

Up to this point, the customer has only agreed to pay for the massage.

After a few minutes of Noi sliding up and down his body, (you will probably not believe this) but some of the more excitable chaps often ask for a little more and are prepared (desperate) to pay for the extras, this being referred to as a "Happy Ending".

Noi had sorted out 5 such adventurous individuals that day and was now sporting a sore pussy. (Her words not mine)

The next evening I was in Little Susy bar telling a couple of friends about the girl, both of whom were amazed that I had never been for the famed Thai oily massage.

"Don't be shy Billy - Noi ready for happy ending."

I have an oily massage every week," said Bob."

"I had one this afternoon," said Steve.

"Clucking Bells," said Billy.

"Let's go now," said Monty

T'was a couple of days later that I accepted Noi's invitation to an oily massage, not at her massage parlour, but back at my hotel, and I was surprised to find that she had brought along Gip, her young lesbian lover.

"Today we do something special," she said.

First we have shower Billy - then we have massage, OK?

Monty not only fulfilled his lifelong ambition of 3 in a bed, both he and I discovered exactly what 2 Lezzies get up to after all those years of wondering – wondering that went right back to the drawings on the toilet wall during my schoolboy days.

Oh my God
- do they
really do
that?

CHAPTER 17
LEK REDISCOVERED

Now living in Thailand does have its downside, one of which is the Thai singing voice. I have finally decided to "come out" and will now officially declare myself a RACIST.

All people are NOT born equal.

The vocal cords of the average Thai girl are countless generations of evolution behind the Western world in their development.

To listen to their screeching rendition of several Thai songs, all of which have the musical complexity of "Three blind mice", is second only to being locked in a darkened room with an asthmatic, drunken Scotsman playing the sabre dance on his bagpipes.

The highlight of any evening is when a dozen of them join in the Karaoke, each one of them singing their own version of three blind mice, all in a different key and all being completely tone-deaf. The baritone section is usually provided by two ladyboys with enormous boobs and an 11-o-clock shadow.

Not all ladyboys look like film stars.

As every Thai in the entire world is totally tone-deaf, they greet each painful version of musical torture with much enthusiasm, while the Farangs (Westerners) cringe and try to escape in the hope that no-one notices.

Lek in working mode down Walking Street

My ears often remain in a tinnitus state of shock for days, and there are times when I wonder if they will ever recover.

One evening, I found myself at such a party with Lek, the adorable creature that I had met on the bus from the airport on my very first day in Thailand.

Being unable to find her bar, I had almost forgotten about her because of my few months with Duane, when quite by chance one evening, Monty suddenly became excited and forcibly dragged me across the Soi Buakhao road, narrowly avoiding a passing motorbike, having spotted her dressed in little more than half a handkerchief and a bra that barely covered her nipples.

Lek was now working as an Agogo dancer in Walking Street, the red-light district of a red-light city, and had wangled a couple of hours off so that she could go to a friend's birthday party in Soi Honey at an inspirationally named bar called "Your Bar".

The party was good, and the female singer with the band hit pretty close to the right note in the right key maybe once or twice in each song.

Even a blind squirrel bumps into the occasional acorn.

Around 10-o-clock, the serious screeching started as the mike was commandeered by several of the 20 or so bar girls at the party, and soon I was longing for the melodic tones of Sgt McTavish's bagpipes.

By 11-30 most of the girls were happily drunk when naturally enough the real action started.

It began with the sound of breaking glass as it always does.

This is accompanied by much shouting and screaming followed by the rapid movement of girls all in the same direction.

I grabbed Lek's arm.

This was pointless, as to try and prevent a Thai girl from fighting often means that all hostilities will temporarily cease, and their violent anger will become directed at you by every damned one of the protagonists.

Once they have beaten you to a pulp, they will resume their gang bang bust-up.

Little did I know at this point that Lek was a black belt in Muay Thai, a particularly dangerous martial art.

Lek in training mode

More glasses were broken and the conflict rapidly escalated, even more girls joining in until there was perhaps an equal number on each side.

It now spilt out onto the road, (Soi Honey) as all 20 girls got stuck into whoever was the closest to them, having completely forgotten which side they were on. Another dozen or so girls from the bar next door joined in.

Traffic came to a halt in both directions, the drivers leaving their cars to watch the action.

This was bloody great entertainment, the best party ever, every participant strictly adhering to the Marquess of Queensberry rules on MMM (Mixed Martial Melee), the only weapons allowed was the prescribed high heeled shoes, beer bottles and bar stools.

Kung Fu kicks and Karate chops accompanied each girl's desire to rip enough hair from her opponent's head as to render her completely bald.

Bar girl
Kung Fu
ballet with
added pain

Someone had called the police as the traffic throughout Pattaya was beginning to back up, and within minutes 2 squad cars arrived. The coppers took one look at the battlefield, got back into their cars and drove off in reverse, knowing full well that if they intervened, all 30 plus girls would turn on them and rip them to pieces before resuming the affray.

A large group of European men from both the party and the bar next door watched the action, and very soon many of the girls were no longer dressed, everything having been torn from their body.

It is impossible to describe a Thai girl's anger.

It isn't something that builds up gradually, it is an uncontrollable nuclear chain reaction type of explosion that is accompanied by a psychopathic desire to kill or maim anything within their line of vision.

Recommended protection during argument with Thai girl

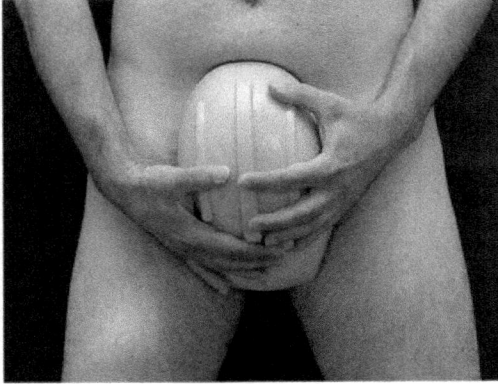

Believe me, all forms of humanity and common sense disappears when the red mist descends, and it is no surprise that Bangkok has the highest rate of dick re-attachment in the world.

No form of decency prevails; anything that comes to hand will be utilized.

It is quite probable that Mrs Bobbit had more than a little Thai blood flowing through her veins as she cut her husband's dick off before driving away and throwing it out of the car window.

(Paddy thought he had hit a mosquito with an enormous dick as it had splattered against his windscreen.)

There was an occasional lull in the battle as the girls became tired, but an argument would soon break out again and hostilities would be resumed, the entire spectacle lasting for almost half an hour.

Lek returned from the fray slightly dishevelled and showing a few scratches. She asked me to tie a knot in the bikini top that had been ripped off her, and being a chivalrous sort of chap, I complied, slowly – very slowly.

Monty and I were again reminded of what great tits and teeth she had.

"You look tired Lek, my darling," I said. "Why don't you come back to my hotel for a massage, that will help you to relax and heal your wounds."

Lek nodded gently.

Monty nodded vigorously almost causing me to lose my balance.

Don't you just love the subservient compliance of a woman after a good scrap?

As we left the bar, Joe and his wife came over, said their good-byes, and thanked us for coming.

"Great party Joe," I said.

"You liked the group then Bill?"

"No, they were shit but the entertainment was first class."

I ducked as his Thai wife aimed a slap at me.

I have to say that this was only one of many fights that I have seen break out among Thai girls, the usual reason being jealousy over customers or boyfriends, as the bargirls prefer to call them, even though their passionate liaison may have lasted for little more than one evening.

Should the Farang fancy a change from the girl who had previously sampled the contents of his wallet, and chose a different girl for the evening, this becomes a loss of face and can easily turn into a catfight, both girls often turning on the poor bloke and attacking him.

Thai girls can be very unpredictable and must always be treated with caution.

CHAPTER 18
LEK REDISCOVERED (2)

Lek moved in with Monty and I after a few days, still keeping in touch with her many overseas boyfriends who continued to send money every month. This is a common arrangement between Thai girls and the lovelorn men who dream of little else but their annual sexual sojourn when they are back home in their cold, wet, and lonely Western world.

One day as we visited her family back in the village, Lek had a motorbike accident and cut her leg so I accompanied her to hospital.

I must point out that the village was unlike the village of the baboon and by Thai standards was fairly upmarket.

Having sat in the hospital waiting room for a couple of hours bored out of my brains, I popped outside to a little open establishment laughingly referred to as a café and tried to order something to eat that was remotely edible.

Monty was completely against it and tried his best to drag me away.

The menu was in Thai, and the owner, cook, cleaner, and dishwasher, walked over and spoke to me in a fluent chimpanzee series of grunts and gargles.

I went oink, oink, at the same time saying pork, he nodded and disappeared in the direction of his kitchen.

Oink
bloody
oink

Any chance of my attempting to learn so much as one word of Thai disappeared when I discovered that the language contained 26 vowels.

When you consider that the average Scouser or Brummie has only ever managed to master no more than 3 of our 5 vowels, and the Welsh have given up completely and replaced all 5 of them with a combination of Y's and L's, you can imagine how difficult it is for an Englishman to get his nonreptile shaped tongue around 26 of the damn things.

Five minutes later a bowl of squid and octopus appeared at the table with no sign whatsoever of any pork. I can only assume that going oink, oink, somehow reminded him of something with tentacles that he had once either caught or eaten.

oink - oink

I viewed the dish with some suspicion, mentally calculating how many seconds it would take me to reach the toilet, open the door, and return the lot of it back into Thai hands in time for the café owner to reheat and serve to the next customer.

Running through my mind was my 2-day agonising experience with my first ever Thai meal at the Pattaya Savoy Grill across the road from my hotel.

Some 30 minutes had passed before the first stirrings were noticed, and the journey back to Lek's house was not without its difficulties.

Volcanic aris syndrome once again laid me low for a couple of days.

Can you check this out doc?

Not only do the Thais eat some rather disgusting creatures and concoctions, occasionally they have some very strange habits and traditions.

This was brought home to me very early on in my relationship with Lek when she asked me along to a lady friend's bar for a Buddhist blessing.

The bar in question is called the Benelux bar and is situated on Soi Buakhao close to the market.

Being slightly hungover after a late night's carousing, I slept in late and turned up at the bar just in time to see a dozen Buddhist monks file in and sit on the floor at the far end of the bar, legs crossed.

The 15 girls that work at the bar did likewise across the room from them.

I sat on the floor and tried to sit the same way, rapidly concluding that a Westerner's legs have been connected to the torso in such a manner as to render the entire operation completely impossible to anyone other than a circus contortionist.

It was as I shuffled around trying to get comfortable that I noticed the delicious aroma of barbecued chicken, and looking at the table in the corner of the room I was delighted to find that the banquet not only contained a selection of creatures, but there was also a mountain of chicken wings and pork.

I was starving and couldn't wait to get started – - but – - we had to get the monking stuff over with, after all, that was the reason that we were there in the first place.

Now, the whole process of the monking bit is extremely confusing to the Western brain.

It is best described by the Thais as a "blessing" for good luck.

When you consider that the bar sells alcohol and the 15 girls sell something else a little more substantial, the mind boggles at the thought of the monks blessing the girls with good luck as they set about their job of checking out the ceiling decoration of various hotel rooms, legs high in the air and a satisfying grin on their faces as they participate in the national sport of Thailand.

After what seemed like hours of chanting and wailing, which to me sounded as unintelligible as a troop of Glaswegians discussing theology; well, Glaswegians discussing anything in fact, the great moment arrived and the girls began to serve the food, placing in front of me an enormous silver platter filled with chicken, pork, and an assortment of fried creatures.

All for me?

Visions of Duane's Udon Thani rat barbecue flashed momentarily before my eyes, as I at first studied, and then mentally visualized the creatures happily hopping, crawling, flying, and swimming around before the boiling fat had turned them into objects of Thai culinary dreams and fantasy.

I felt quite proud really, as the girls had handed the monks small portions of food on paper plates, while I had this whacking great silver platter, so naturally enough I assumed that I was the guest of honour and not these old guys dressed in their saffron robes.

I steadied myself, starving hungry and anxiously waiting for the monks to begin eating.

At last, the monking stopped and the chomping started.

I set about the task of demolishing any food on the platter that I could recognize as being edible.

There was a sudden hush.

The eating stopped.

Everyone in the room was staring at me.

The silver platter was not for me – it wasn't for anyone – at least not for anyone mortal.

How was I to know that each item on the enormous silver platter represented a dead relative of someone in the room and I had just eaten the bar owner's granddad and Lek's aunty Wong?

Strangely, I have never been invited to a bar blessing since, and Fah, the Thai lady who owns the bar, hasn't spoken a word to me for over 7 years. Apparently, she really loved her granddad – so did I, he was delicious.

Aunty Wong, however, was a little too spicy and must have been pretty hot stuff and one hell of a bar girl in her mortal days.

Strange people – even stranger traditions.

After the feast, Lek, having replaced my silver platter with a paper plate containing only edible items with no ghostly symbolism, the Monks resumed their monking, the head honcho walking round to each girl in turn and tapping them on the head with a stick that he had dipped in water.

When he got to me, instead of a tap, he swung the stick and nearly knocked my head off, obviously upset that I had just broken with Thai tradition and eaten all those dead people.

Lek was kneeling beside me and I said. "Tell him that monk or no bloody monk, if he does that again I'm going to deck him."

He seemingly understood English and backed away.

Buddha was obviously observing proceedings and decided to join forces with Lucifer to forever blight my life from there onwards.

My mind drifted back some 30 or so years when I still ran my Wolvey fishery and I was at Meadowlands Fishery on the outskirts of Coventry talking to my good friend John Bloor.

Now it has oft been rumoured that occasionally, I can be a taker of the Michael, Mrs McEnroe, my pet name for John's wife being one of my favourite targets.

Mrs McEnroe ran a little food stall at the fishery, and every week I would phone her and give her the number of people admitted to Walsgrave hospital with food poisoning that week as a result of eating her burgers.

One day I turned up at Meadowlands to see John and asked the good lady for a burger.

She glared, said something extremely unpleasant and fried up the burger, which was served on a nice white serviette.

"Not one word or I will hit you with the frying pan," came the threat.

I smiled condescendingly and proceeded to demolish the burger, making all the appropriate yums, accompanied by much lip licking.

"Delicious", I said. "Absolutely fabulous, the best burger I have ever eaten".

Mrs McEnroe was delighted.

I then reached into my pocket and took out a box of Rennies, emptied around 20 into my hand and stuffed the lot into my mouth, chomping and crunching them in front of her.

Mrs McEnroe turned red and reached for the frying pan.

It was perhaps 2 weeks later that I had to pop over to Meadowland again to see John.

Mrs McEnroe shot daggers from her eyes.

"One of your delicious burgers please".

"Bugger off".

"Please, please, I promise no more tricks and I won't say a word".

"If you do, I will wrap this frying pan around your head".

"Scouts honour, not a word".

Five minutes later, the burger was served on a neat white serviette, and Mrs McEnroe stood very close, pan in hand.

"Ketchup and mustard please".

Pan still in hand, she passed them over and stood open-mouthed as I neatly squirted both ketchup and mustard all around the burger.

I then picked up the burger, threw it in the bin and ate the serviette.

Mrs McEnroe's eyes blinked, opened wide; and then crossed maniacally before turning murderous.

The first swipe missed me by a few inches, at which point John and I rediscovered our youthful athletic ability.

Hell hath no fury like a burger frying Prima Donna scorned.

CHAPTER 19
IT'S ONLY BUSINESS

I have mentioned that Lek had 3 boyfriends on the go at the same time as she was living with me and attempting to describe both Pattaya and the bar girls that live and work in the city is difficult when the whole process is judged by Western standards. There are occasions when you simply must stand back in admiration at the guile, cunning, and innovative ingenuity of some of the girls.

Take on board the very real oft-spoken phrase.

"THERE IS NO FOOL LIKE AN OLD FOOL."

Nowhere in the world is this more applicable than in Pattaya, and it was brought home to me one afternoon when Lek informed me that she would be away on business for a couple of weeks.

Neither Monty nor I liked it, but the blunt reality was that each of her 3 boyfriends sent her 500 quid every month which would certainly guarantee her fidelity. Each of the OLD FOOLS honestly thought that she would go back to the village and keep her legs tightly crossed for 50 weeks until they returned for their annual 2 weeks lovefest and gymnastics.

To begin with, a European, Scandinavian, American, Canadian, or Australian man (all known to Thai girls as Farangs), pops over to Pattaya for a couple of week's holiday knowing exactly what he wants, having heard all the tales about the place.

I would guess that the average age of these holidaymakers is well in excess of 50, possible around 60, with many being in their

70's.

The object of their desire will probably average around 25 but can range anywhere from 18 to 40ish.

The problem arises when "THE OLD FOOL" in him kicks in, and after a few days in the company of the same candy bar he begins to fall in love – the candy bar in question will immediately recognize the signs and also "fall in love", despite in many cases THE OLD FOOL resembling a Sumo wrestler who has let himself go and bought a pie shop.

Old fool and candy bar

At this point, the open wallet surgery begins.

When the holiday ends, considerably poorer and broken-hearted, the love-struck 60-year-old Farang returns to his home-land promising faithfully to send his only true love a fair amount of money each month until his return to Pattaya to resume the love affair.

The candy bar then returns to her original bar and resumes work.

I'm pretty sure that you can see what is coming next.

Over the course of a year, the prettier and more convincing

candy bars manage to have several "OLD FOOLS" fall in love with them, all of whom will be sending them money monthly, and all of whom will be desperate to return to Pattaya to resume their relationship with the only girl in the world for them.

Pattaya girls are resourceful if nothing else, and Lek, one of the more beautiful sirens, was horrified to find that 2 of her Sugar Daddies were both arriving on the same plane from the change-over airport of Bahrain; each one bearing gifts, and with the aid of copious amounts of Viagra would once again resume their undying love affair.

Lek had to come up with a cunning plan and had to do an awful lot of complicated juggling and lying, otherwise, a large slice of her monthly income was in jeopardy.

On arrival in Bangkok, Sugar Daddies 1 and 2 each received a phone call with a different set of instructions.

Waw, the viagra really does work

Number 1 was to meet her at a hotel out of town, while numbers 2 was informed that her mother had been rushed to the hospital way up North in her village and Lek had caught the overnight bus to visit her.

She then arranged for one of her girlfriends to "entertain" number 2 for a few days until she supposedly "returned".

Later in the evening, number 2 received a tearful phone call pleading for money to pay for her mother's hospital bills. The OLD FOOL duly obliged by transferring several hundred pounds into her bank account.

After 3 days with number 1, she then informed him that her mother was seriously ill and that she would need money to pay her hospital bills.

Number 1 duly obliged, so she kissed him and bade him farewell as she now had to go up to the village to see her mother – one hour later, she met up with number 2 and her girlfriend transferred her affections over to number 1.

I'm getting a little confused with numbers now, but I am sure that you can see how the rather slick operation works.

The OLD FOOLS were by now almost tearful at poor Lek's plight, each one of them enjoying her favours for brief spells of 2 or 3 days, punctuated by equally productive spells with her girlfriend, and at the end of their holiday had been completely taken in by the well-crafted deception, each of them paying Lek another great wad of cash to pay for her mother's funeral, the poor old crone having supposedly croaked.

They then climbed onto the same plane back to Bahrain and onward to Heathrow completely unaware of each other's existence, and each of them continuing to send the only girl in the world, the loving and completely faithful Lek, her monthly allowance.

And Lek's dead mother?

Still enjoying lots of bones

Fit as a butcher's dog and still successfully catering for the needs of Farangs that prefer the more mature ladies.

Monty was over the moon when Lek returned and listened attentively as she recounted and re-enacted details of her lost fortnight.

I lost interest and went to sleep leaving them to it.

It was a few weeks later that I heard of a bit of banging in the bedroom and discovered Lek packing her suitcase.

"Solly Billy," she said tearfully. "My boyfriend in Korea want me melly (marry) and he velly rich.

Monty was distraught

He and Lek had been inseparable for the past few weeks.

Lek left to pursue her pot of gold and a forlorn Monty and I poured ourselves a drink.

Life wasn't really that bad.

Lek and Duane had been just two of the 100,000 girls that work the city.

There were 99,998 still to be explored.

CHAPTER 20
DIE FARANG – DIE

It was now April, and at last, the great FESTIVAL OF THE CULL was upon us here in Thailand.

For those people not familiar with the country, it is known as Songkran, the world's greatest water festival. In reality, it is a Government inspired exercise in counteracting the overzealous sexual antics of the Thai female population by sanctioning 9 days of frantic road traffic culling.

Now firstly you need to know the unbreakable rules before taking part in the cull.

Rule 1 — You will need a motorbike. Everyone has one, so if you are on holiday you can hire one for the day. It will be pointless hiring one for more than one day as the likelihood of you still being alive at the end of the day is remote.

Rule 2 — Under no circumstances must you mount the motorbike if you can stand for more than 10 seconds without falling over or see an oncoming vehicle more than 5 yards away. Drugs may be used but the best part of a bottle of cheap Thai whisky is the Government recommendation and the course most usually followed by all Thais, both male and female.

Random breathalyser tests are taken, and anyone found guilty of being sober will be deported.

Rule 3 — Crash helmets and all other forms of protection are strictly forbidden and will certainly lead to your disqualification from the cull and possible arrest if found cheating.

Rule 4 — It is important to check the local speed limit as you will be expected to drive at least double that figure regardless of other road users.

Rule 5 — You will score extra points for every passenger that you are carrying on the bike, 1 being the absolute minimum and 5 being the upper limit.

Into battle - water guns and buckets ready

Now as in all good games you need opponents.

These will be found in the form of some 100,000 scantily clad Thai bar girls who will be stood outside every bar hurling buckets of iced water in your face as you drive by, loudly applauding and cheering every accident that they manage to cause. You, in turn, will be expected to let go of the handlebars and cover your eyes, as many of the buckets will have ice cubes in them for maximum skin penetration.

Isn't this fun - now die

Am I joking?

Perhaps I am exaggerating a little but not by much I can assure you; anyone who has lived through the 9 days of carnage that is Pattaya at Songkran will confirm that the above roughly sums up the situation.

Hundreds of people die during Songkran every year and many thousands are injured, almost all of them being motorbike accidents caused by drink, drugs, and buckets of iced water in the face.

The above government inspired culling exercise really must be applauded, as, without the festival, the Thais would by now probably outnumber the Chinese because of their obsession with their national sport of incessant procreation.

It was on the 3rd day of my first Songkran festival that I staggered into Benelux bar on Soi Buakhao, the same bar where I had been attacked by the psychotic monk when I had been with Lek.

The previous evening I had met up with a couple of old mates from my match fishing days at Little Susy bar and had just spent the entire afternoon with them, flitting from bar to bar and dodging buckets of iced water.

I stopped dead in my tracks.

I had been warned that when living in Thailand 2 golden rules must never be broken.

Rule 1 — Do not fall in love.

Rule 2 — Do not buy a bar.

Someone walked towards me.

My eyes glazed over and my vision became blurred.

It was too late.

I had broken rule 1 and I hadn't yet even made it inside the bar.

Monty became frozen in time, unable to even speak – he was in good company as neither could I.

At that one point in time, it became blindly apparent that most of the 100,000 unfortunate Pattaya bar girls would never get to experience the sublime, mentally and physically attuned partnership that Monty and I had developed into.

I had just met Rinda, and the hedonistic days and nights of carousing and tarting had to end.

Bloody hell – I had decided to grow up and I still hadn't got to the bar counter.

Some 15 minutes later, as I stood with Rinda by the pool table, beer in hand, there suddenly came a scream from behind the bar. Fah, the owner, recognised me as the Farang who had eaten her granddad a few weeks earlier during the mad monk's blessing and attacked me with a bottle.

Get out –
you ate
my grandad

I left quickly – very quickly.

Fortunately, I had taken Rinda's phone number and was able to contact her early the next evening.

Three months later I broke rule number 2 and bought a bar.

Rinda had joined the partnership, and Monty enthusiastically welcomed her with open arms.

Duane and Lek were now distant memories.

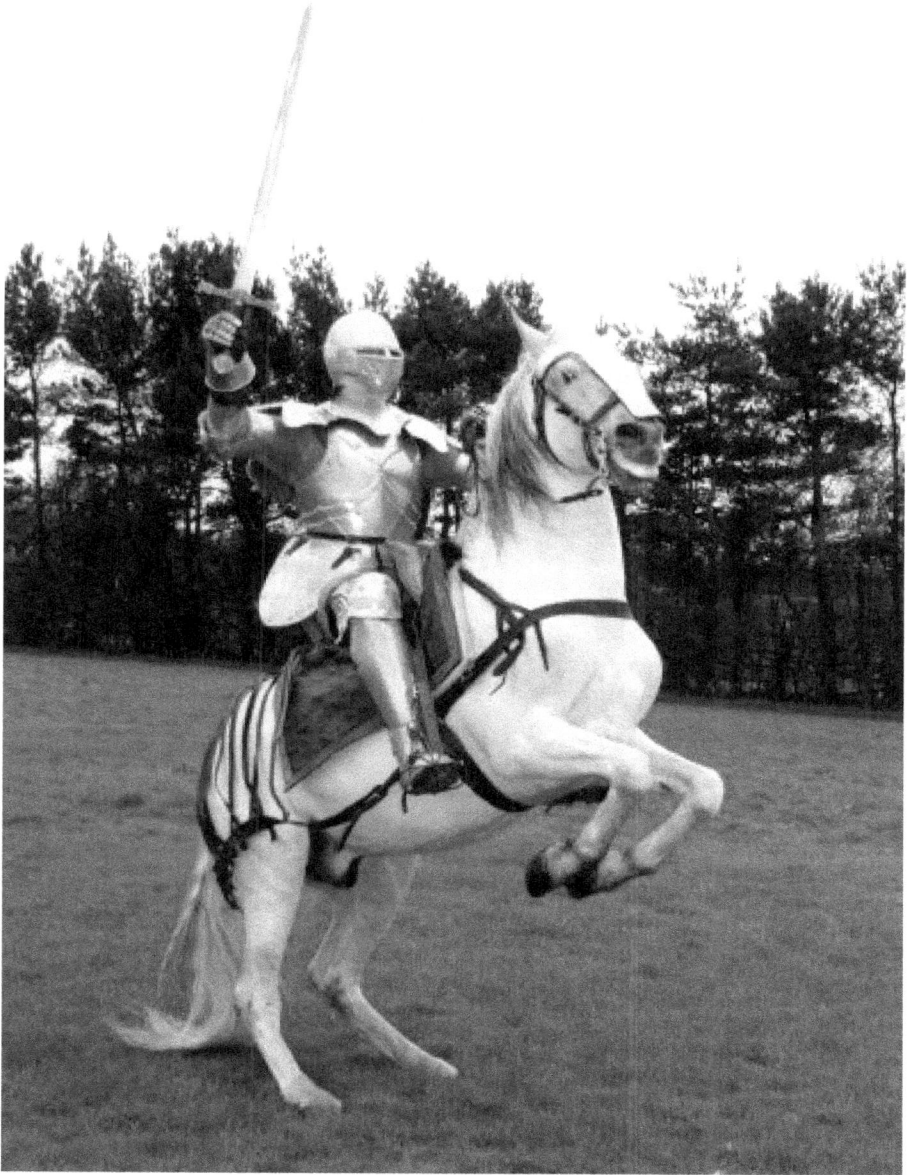

Monty was back in the saddle.

CHAPTER 21
RINDA

Now Rinda was unlike any Thai girl that I had yet come across.

Rinda had a brain, something that set her apart from the rest of the girls in Pattaya.

She hadn't had the easiest of lives, having been dogged by more than her fair share of bad luck together with a complete lack of opportunity in the village farming environment where she had been brought up.

The family had been middle class in Thai village terms, her father being both a shop owner and a hitman, with a rumoured 50 hits to his credit, mostly commissioned by the Bangkok Mafia.

He got careless with one of his paid hits one evening.

Being drunk, he shot an off-duty policeman by mistake and served 11 years in prison – this happening when Rinda hadn't yet entered her teens.

I often wondered whether the disappearance of the family fortune was in some way linked to him avoiding the death penalty and receiving a relatively short sentence, but never pressed

Rinda on this point.

The family were now no longer middle class, in fact, they were broke, and Rinda had to ride the family motorbike to the market every morning to collect vegetables, meat, and fresh stock for the shop before going to school; this beginning at the age of 11.

Shopping before school

Why didn't her 2 brothers help?

To begin with, they were much too young, still, it must be pointed out that as a rule, Thai men are bone idle and everything falls on the daughter. This is very much traditional in Thai families, and every one of my bar girls sends money home to look after the family while their husbands, fathers, and brothers, lounge around drinking and playing cards.

Rinda married her Thai boyhood sweetheart shortly after obtaining her university degree, and like many Thai men he very soon developed the "stick your dick in anything with a pulse" mentality, dying in a Songkran motorbike accident shortly after Rinda had managed to divorce him.

Rinda became a schoolteacher earning the going rate of 150 pounds a month, not really enough to pay the mortgage on the house that she and her husband had just built, nor to bring up a son – Rinda was now pregnant.

Her chemistry degree helped her into a pharmaceutical company management position where she ran her own department, but still, there wasn't enough of a salary to pay the family bills, her brothers as always contributing sod all and her mother having the brains of a newt.

Her father had died of alcohol poisoning shortly after leaving prison and returning home.

A family friend gave her a tip-off that there was good money to be made illegally running diesel into the country from Malaya, so she packed in her job, borrowed some money, bought a truck, and made the 1,500-mile trip to the Thai / Malay border.

The friend had been right, the money was good, the risks, however, were quite high, and she had to hide the truck in jungle clearings on more than one occasion, sat alone with all the lights switched off all through the night until the border patrols went away.

Having been picked up and fortunately let off a couple of times, a compromise was reached with the border patrol chief. As is the way with everything in the Far East, a bribe smooths away all problems, and soon she was making the border crossing several times a day and earning pretty good money.

The only flaw in the system was the fact that for many of the people that live in Thailand, evolution has somehow bypassed the organ known as the brain and has replaced it with something the size and shape of a baked bean.

The guards got greedy and began demanding ever bigger bribes until Rinda's enterprise was no longer commercially viable.

Rinda jumped into her truck, drove towards the bright lights of Pattaya and was now living with Monty and me.

"From now on girl," I told her. "Things will only go in one direction, and that direction is up."

Rinda was ambitious and longed for her own bar, so 3 months later we bought the Dragon bar off Freddy, a lovely bloke who for the first week gave us both useful advice on how to run the place.

We spent a bit of money on modifications and converted 2 of the larger bedrooms into 4 smaller ones for the girls to live in.

Now came the recruitment.

Rinda's village had dozens of lithe young girls who were only too eager to sample the delights of Pattaya rather than be standing ankle-deep in the Paddy fields, planting and cutting rice. Soon, she had assembled a decent stable of leggy fillies who were both surprised and delighted to find that "rich" Farangs were only too willing to pay for what the lads and dads of the village had been getting for free ever since the onset of puberty.

Home time after a hot day in the rice fields

Rinda, Monty, and I were now up and running, Monty ever eager to begin the training of every new filly on arrival and being amazed to find that he himself was usually on the receiving end of the training.

The Thai National Sport had produced a stable of world-class sexual athletes and it was now time for me to keep my promise to Rinda.

CHAPTER 22
UP AND RUNNING

First comes the theory

SCHOOL FOR BAR-GIRLS

I DON'T UNDERSTAND......   HANDSOME MAN......
GRANDMA'S SICK......   HEY ! LONG HAIR......
BROTHER FALL OFF MOTORBIKE......   YOUR LOVELY......
I NOT VELLY WELL......   WHERE YOU STAY......
I STAY AT FRIENDS HOUSE......   I LOVE YOU. DAR-LINK......
I GO HOME FOR TWO DAYS.   HOW LONG YOU STAY......
IT WASN'T ME......   WHAT HOTEL YOU STAY......
I VIRGIN,I ONLY HAVE ONE BABY......   FAT BELLY, NO PROBLEM......
I GO WITH YOU......   YOU SEXY MAN......
YOUR FRIEND ME......   I LIKE CHOCOLATE......
I HAVE NO MONEY......   I NO BUTTERFLY......
I NO HAVE THAI BOYFRIEND......   I WAIT FOR YOU......
BUY ME DINK......   OH ! YOU VELLY BIG......
YOU CHEAP CHARLIE......   I NEVER FORGET YOU......
MY BANK ACCOUNT NUMBER IS......   BUY ME GOLD......

M.J.B.

www.mikebairdcartoonist.simplesite.com

Then the practical.

Next please girls

Boot camp finished
- practical training finished -
job well done Monty

Barry occasionally
helps Monty with
the practical training

Karl and
Ashley
also lend
a hand

Did I pass Monty? Have I got the job?

Owning a bar in Pattaya, whilst appearing to be akin to having been deposited smack bang in the middle of Fantasy Island with more than enough totty to shake your stick at, does have its downsides, the main one being the question of fidelity.

I soon got to know many of the Farang bar owners, and the temptation of being surrounded by thousands of gorgeous young women, many of whom were in their employ, is often simply too much for most of them to resist.

This is where the problems begin.

Most of the bar owners have either a wife or girlfriend in tow, all of whom are endowed with a psychotic approach to absolute fidelity. Their farang partner becomes THEIR property, and any form of playing away from home can be dangerous. I have already mentioned that Bangkok has the highest rate of dick reattachment in the world, so one simple indiscretion can easily result in the voice being raised by a couple of octaves.

The girls have also created a form of sisterhood, comprising of a network of bar girl spies, all of whom are only too willing to become either super grasses or double agents.

For this reason, many ingenious methods of deception have evolved to enable the bar owners to sample the same physical delights that they, in turn, provide for their customers, while at the same time providing their main source of income in their bars.

Charlie owns a bar a hundred or so yards from the Dragon bar, and every Friday night he goes walkabout around town with a few of his bar customers, always popping into a certain Agogo bar in Soi Metro where he meets up with a particularly beautiful pole dancer for a bit of "how's your father?"

He buys his customers a drink, makes his excuses, and disappears upstairs for half an hour.

This discrete approach worked well enough for a couple of months until one fateful Friday when Charlie was struck down by Thai volcanic aris syndrome, having foolishly sampled no more than a mouthful of his wife's cooking.

Thai volcanic
aris syndrome
and Charlie

At home, alone in his bed and feeling extremely sorry for himself, he had to ring his Agogo girl to explain his non-appearance, and as she wasn't particularly busy, they began a rather physically stimulating conversation culminating in both parties taking and sending photos of their most secret anatomical parts.

It was perhaps a week or so later that the girls at Charlie's bar were laughing and giggling at the images that were being passed around and posted onto every girl's phone.

That is disgusting - does anyone have his phone number?

Charlie's dick was becoming quite an international celebrity, and its image began to cross the Thai border and travel throughout Asia.

The image was also transferred to the phone of Pim, Charlie's wife, who after laughing along with the other girls looked a little more carefully at the dick that was now smiling and waving at her.

She zoomed in on a barely noticeable photograph in the background and recognised the two figures.

It was Charlie and Pim's wedding photograph that was innocently sitting on the dressing table beside the bed.

With a face like thunder and screaming "I'm going to cut his xxxxx dick off," she grabbed the knife used for slicing the lemons at the bar, jumped on her motorbike, and set off with evil and malicious intent.

Fortunately for Charlie, one of his bar girls recognised the problem, together with Pim's evil and malicious intent, and rang to inform him of the out-of-control tsunami heading in his direction.

Not wishing to become the next Mr Bobbit, Charlie came and stayed with me for a couple of days until the heat died down.

Rinda, in turn, took great delight in sharpening a knife in front of the pair of us, a threatening smile appearing as she nonchalantly chopped a cucumber in half.

Close
your eyes
Charlie,
this is
going
to hurt

Monty got the message loud and clear.

Bargirl training was suspended indefinitely.

Charlie also got the message, and any future indiscretions were conducted well away from Pattaya, the usual place being Ban Chang – more later.

CHAPTER 23
THIS IS THAILAND

Now Adam, another English bar owner, wasn't quite so fortunate and barely managed to survive the fate of Mr Bobbit by seconds.

Nan, his girlfriend, was even more jealous that the average Thai girl and believe me, that is seriously bad.

She had a few drinks too many one night and noticed him paying a little too much attention to one of the bar girls in his employ.

A marble ashtray violently smashed into the back of his head and his business talk with the girl ended abruptly 5 minutes before the ambulance arrived to take him to hospital.

Little more than a couple of weeks later, a once again drunken Nan heard a whisper that Adam had been playing away from home, so she promptly left the bar and paid 3 motorbike taxi men to beat him up.

That came to nothing as the first 2 attackers hit the floor unconscious and the third one ran away.

Unfortunately for them, Nan had forgotten to tell them how big Adam was.

Undeterred, the next time she chose her moment a little more carefully.

Adam awoke from what appeared to be a violent nightmare to find Nan sawing away at his most prized possession and the root of his problem with what was, fortunately, a fairly blunt carving knife.

Once again, the ambulance arrived and took him to the hospital, where a skilled surgeon reassembled the half-dead dick and inserted several stitches to stop it dropping off.

ADAM'S EYES BEGAN TO WATER

I don't know if Adam will follow the same route as Mr Bobbit, who had his sewn back on and became a porn star, but having got rid of Nan, he has certainly been rehearsing for future stardom with great gusto.

I mentioned the incident to a couple of my bar girls who confirmed that such a punishment for a wayward husband is quite common practice here in Thailand; Monty screamed out loud, and to this day there are no carving knives in the house that Rinda, Monty and I share.

I was in the doghouse as I wandered through the mean streets of Pattaya, a lost soul, a sheep without its' shepherd.

Why had God deserted me?

I was innocent.

Rinda, my one and only true love, (Fishing excluded) had banned me from both of my bars.

My crime had been fabricated; it was no more than an illusion.

It was smoke and mirrors.

I had not committed any form of indiscretion with the lovely, dark-eyed, nubile, long-legged, well-endowed Lek Lek at my bar.

It was her hand that had strayed, not mine.

I had told her quite clearly that I would become very angry indeed if it was still hovering around and occasionally caressing my groin in ten minutes time.

Monty interrupted and insisted on 15 minutes.

Rinda saw things differently - that was why I was now banned from both of my bars.

In a slightly alcoholic haze, I stumbled into Fubar, a favourite watering hole of mine, and sitting in the corner that is exclusively reserved for sociopaths and ex-pats in the terminal stages of sexual deviancy and depravity, were Adam and Jimmy McJimbo.

Jimmy McJimbo told his story.

He had been out for a session, and, as one does in Pattaya after a few drinks, decided to bar fine and take out a particularly pretty bar girl.

He got lucky.

Instead of retiring to a local hotel, this rather sexy lass had her own house in a district of Pattaya that is known as the dark side.

Barely sober, Jimmy McJimbo went to work and found that he was now in the inexhaustible clutches of every man's dream, a rampant nymphomaniac.

Totally exhausted after some 2- or 3-minutes feverish exertion, Jimmy McJimbo made his rather feeble excuses and fell into a deep erotic sleep, dreaming of flocks, herds, shoals, and buckets full of nubile nymphomaniacs.

The morning sun was flickering and dancing through the bedroom blinds as a still pretty drunk Jimmy McJimbo awoke.

This girl really was a goer.

She ticked all the boxes and more.

His eyes were still closed in ecstasy as her tongue slid up and down his now wide awake wee Scottish manhood.

This was without any shadow of a doubt the best sex he had ever experienced.

The tongue lingered, tingled, titillated, teased.

'I've brought you a cup of tea." The voice said.

Jimmy McJimbo opened his eyes and standing in front of him with a cuppa was the girl.

His tiny Scottish brain suddenly clicked into gear – if the girl was standing by the bed, how could she possibly be ???????

He looked down and lying on the bed alongside him with a tongue like a giraffe was the girl's puppy.

Jimmy McJimbo was appalled.

Yes, even Glaswegians have standards.

"Jimmy!" The girl screamed. "You perverted Scottish git; what are you doing with my baby Fido?"

Jimmy drank his tea in one gulp, got dressed and paid the girl 20 quid for the 2 minutes of exertion he had managed before falling asleep.

"How much for the dog?" He said as he left the house, ducking and narrowly avoiding the flying cup and saucer.

How was it for you Jimmy?

Now one day, Jimmy McJimbo found himself quite attracted to a girl who showed a little promise in the intellectual department, having heard of a small island called America somewhere close to Scotland, and took up residence with her after an extended period of road testing a never-ending fleet of Pattaya bar girls.

A couple of weeks into their relationship, Jimmy was tucking into sausage and chips that he had just cooked when his girl asked, "do you like sausages Jimmy?"

"Love em." came the reply.

This was a loving, caring girl, not just a Bimbo with extensive geographical knowledge, and 2 days later a large box arrived at Jimmy's apartment.

He opened it to find a present of 120 sausages, bought by his admiring lover. The fridge was stacked to overflowing and not wishing to upset her, he gave her all the necessary thanks and praises.

He began eating three meals a day of sausages and Viagra and little else.

One week later, Jimmy took his beloved out to a local bar and ordered pie and chips, needing to have a break from the sausages, which he was by now beginning to hate.

"Do you like pies Jimmy?" she asked.

Now you would have thought that something would have set the alarm bells ringing.

"Love pies." said Jimmy, as he devoured the only meal for a whole week that didn't have sausages as the main course.

This week an even bigger box arrived at Jimmy's apartment which took 2 people to carry upstairs.

As I left the bar, Jimmy casually remarked. "If you know anyone with an extra-large chest freezer for sale Billy, ask them to give me a ring."

Delivery for Mr McJimbo

CHAPTER 24
THAI BUILDERS

It was with growing interest that I observed the workers putting on the roof of a building opposite my bar.

I have mentioned it before, but it is a useful warning against mixing up the jobs of the sexes.

Now I don't profess to be a structural engineer, however, there appeared to be something amiss with the way that they went about it, yet I couldn't quite put my finger on it.

All the beams were in place and the necessary steel matting was carefully positioned ready for the concrete pour; still, it didn't look quite right.

The truck arrived and several tons of concrete poured and levelled.

So far so good.

Ten days later, the workers returned to take down the hundred or so bamboo poles that were supporting the roof. I would guess that half of the poles had been removed before a scream rang out, and a dozen men and women began running for their lives.

The entire roof came down within seconds, bodies diving in every direction and disappearing in a cloud of concrete dust.

I then realized what had been the problem.

Despite the roof having enough steel to sink a battleship, no one had considered tying it all in together, with the result that several tons of concrete were supported by 3 inches of concrete without any re-enforcement.

Anyway, no-one got hurt and my bar customers had a good

afternoon's entertainment.

What was very noticeable was the fact that none of the men actually did anything during the construction phase, all the manual work being done by women. Now I'm not suggesting that the whole debacle was the women's fault, however, certain things should be left to men and there are certain tasks that only a woman is genetically programmed to perform - having kids and house cleaning being the most obvious.

Thai women in particular have an uncanny ability to multi-task, being able to breathe, blink, and eat all at the same time.

If they are required to perform any other task, one of the above three functions has to be sacrificed; if they are required to think, then all three have to be suspended; this is very noticeable in my bar when a customer approaches the cashier in order to pay his bar bill.

The cashier holds her breath, closes her eyes, and stops chewing on the dog shit flavoured cud that masquerades as Thai cuisine.

If I had ever given my pet American Pit Bull terrier Thai food for dinner, I would not be alive to tell the tale.

Now I have to be perfectly fair and unbiased regarding the inherent abilities of the female of the species as there are in fact certain tasks that men not only do not want to do, but tasks that men can never do no matter how much thought or coaching goes into the process.

One such task is the operation of the most sinister device ever created by mankind - the automatic washing machine.

Why would a large spinning white bucket have 20 flashing buttons on it and require 4 different types of powder or liquid to do what women used to do with a couple of stones down the local stream?

It was a couple of years ago that Rinda and I moved into our chalet in Pattaya, where we inherited a state-of-the-art washing machine from Billy Banjo, the previous tenant. This monument to man's ingenuity sat outside the chalet on a large terrace over-looking the swimming pool and was soon effortless put to use by Rinda despite having an array of lights and buttons to rival Mission Control in Texas.

The problem occurred with Rinda having to drive the few hundred miles north to her village of Phetchabun in order to sort out a family affair between her equatorial rain forest canopy dwelling relatives.

I was running out of clothes, and for the first time in my life, I entered the forbidden domain of the female of the species and approached the dreaded washing machine.

It all looked simple enough, bung in the clothes, add a bit of powder and press a few buttons.

What could possibly go wrong?

In went the clothes but I couldn't find any powder, so I dropped in a bar of soap instead, then I remembered that she kept the liquid powder in a container under the sink in the kitchen.

Out came a sealed packet of liquid powder and into the machine went the whole contents of the packet. It was then that I noticed that it wasn't washing powder, but was in fact washing up liquid, and I had now emptied into the machine one pint of fairy soap dishwashing liquid.

Undaunted, I closed the door, pressed a few buttons, and as the machine started to make a humming noise, I went indoors to watch the football completely forgetting about the washing for a couple of hours.

As the game ended, I walked out onto the terrace to discover that the washing machine was no longer tethered to its moorings and was running and jumping around the terrace like a bleedin lunatic.

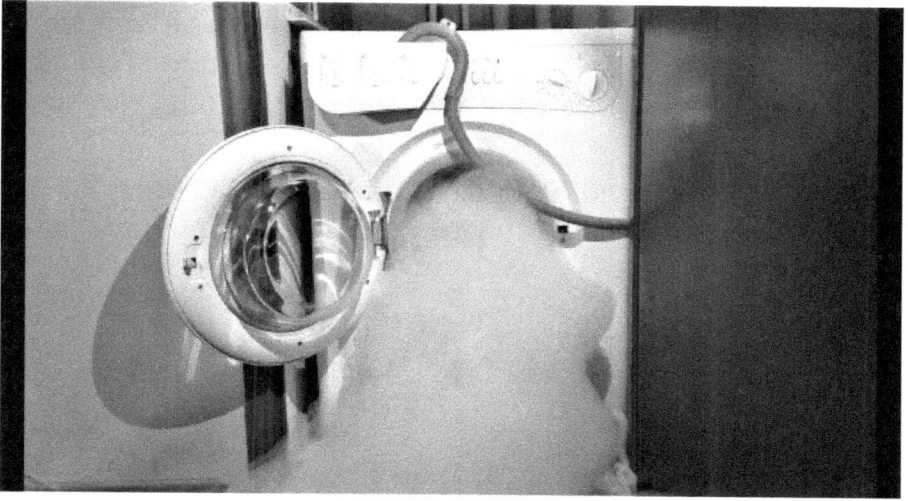

Never mess with women's things.

I grabbed hold of it to stop it shaking, at which point it physically attacked me.

I was now frantically pressing buttons, which only seemed to make it even madder, and it began shaking ever more violently so I opened the door.

What happened next is difficult to describe, but I was suddenly engulfed in an explosion of foam and bubbles.

The damned thing stopped shaking as the pressure had been released, instead, it concentrated its effort on trying to drown me. Soon, the entire balcony disappeared under a sea of bubbles as I groped around blindly searching for the plug.

The machine continued to spin out of control and spew out foam and bubbles at an ever-increasing rate like something out of a science fiction movie.

I could hear people around the pool laughing uncontrollably, but I couldn't see a damned thing as the foam was now over 6 feet high and beginning to spill over the terrace and make its way towards the swimming pool.

Eventually, I managed to pull the electric plug and immobilise the bloody thing, by which time the foam had spotted the open chalet door, engulfing half of the living room on its way to the bedroom.

When Rinda returned from her jungle sojourn, her first job was to bung her clothes in the washing machine and to press a few buttons.

Nothing happened.

"No idea what's wrong darling," I said. "I haven't touched it."

It never worked again.

There are things in life that are not to be messed with – drunken Scotsmen, rattlesnakes, and women's things are perhaps the most obvious.

CHAPTER 25
BAN CHANG

Now one of the favourite ploys for ex-pats wishing to experience a little extra marital indiscretion without their partners finding out is to be found some 30 minutes away from Pattaya at a town called Ban Chang.

The words Ban Chang however are never spoken and are like a red rag to a bull for Pattaya girls; instead, Farangs simply say BC in hushed tones.

WHAT GOES OFF IN BAN CHANG STAYS IN BAN CHANG.

Discretion is pretty much guaranteed.

The Pattaya bar girl spy network that entraps most husbands and boyfriends who like the occasional stray candy bar, is excluded and banned from BC town.

Fortunately, there is a good golf course close to the town and many of the Pattaya golf societies quite magically just happen to arrange a trip there at least once a month.

Unlike Pattaya, which only comes alive in the night, Ban Chang thrives on afternoon trade, and so once a month many golf societies arrange an early kick off and shortly after lunch the members descend on the BC bars.

Ban Chang girls are a little different to Pattaya girls.

Ban Chang girls tend to do whatever you ask them to do while they are still in the bar, a little money providing the necessary incentive that lubricates and removes all inhibitions.

I hadn't been in Pattaya very long (this was pre-Duane), when I finished my early golf round, jumped onto the Golf Society bus, and 10 minutes later found myself sat in a Ban Chang bar with half a dozen fellow golfers, the rest of the party having gone to their own favourite bar in pursuit of their own favourite girl.

"You buy me drink handsome man?" said a quite exquisite candy bar called Mia, who was dressed only in a revealing white 2-piece top and bottom.

I gulped and nodded.

"Thank you." she said. "You like me?"

My eyes popped out as she undid the buttons of her flimsy top.

"You want to see more Billy boy?"

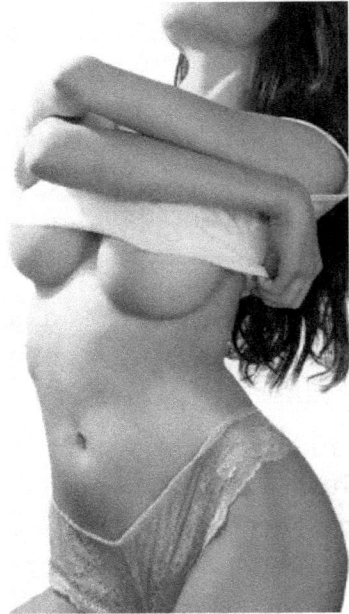

I tried to speak – nothing came out except Monty, who was straining at the leash to get a closer look.

I nodded my head slowly – Monty nodded vigorously.

Mia smiled and patted him lovingly for several seconds, completely ignoring me, the one who had just paid for her drink.

There were times when Monty completely forgot the rules of etiquette and occasionally strained our friendship to the limit.

She listened
to Monty,
not me

Off came the top together with the skirt.

She was now down to a thin blue thong.

I really was taken aback, as having a girl strip almost completely naked in full view of everyone in the bar and then plonk herself on my lap seemed a little too much too quick for someone who had only recently escaped from the clutches of too many sober years of marriage.

I dug deep into my memory bank and honestly couldn't remember this sort of thing ever happening to me in my local pub back home in England.

I wondered why not?

I looked around.

I was feeling a little embarrassed and didn't need to be.

Three of the other golfers each had a completely naked girl sitting on their lap.

I began to warm to the charms of Ban Chang.

Monty was in his seventh heaven.

Now Darren was a big softy who enjoyed a drink, and many an early morning saw the two of us staggering home a little worse for wear.

Darren's sex life had become non-existent, Lun, the 25-year-old 40 kilo girl that he had married 15 years earlier now weighed well north of 70 kilos and only broke off eating so that she could either nag or threaten him.

"I'm thinking of buying myself an inflatable doll." Darren sounded serious.

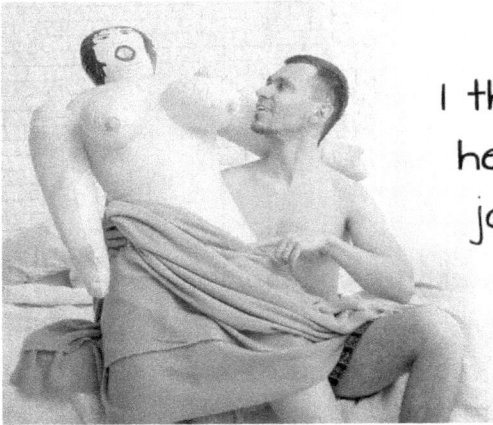

I thought he was joking

"Why don't you come to Ban Chang with the Golf Society on Friday?" I said that evening after a few drinks. "You will have a great time."

"I don't think that Lun would like that Billy, she knows about Ban

Chang, anyway, I haven't played golf for years."

Darren was afraid of Lun; only 3 months earlier during an argument over one particular late night's carousing in bad company, (can't think who that would have been with) she had hurled a plate at him which had smashed his precious flat screen TV, forcing him to spend a king's ransom on a new 45-inch smart TV.

Lun in combative mode

Anyway, I finally persuaded him, and that Friday afternoon, after a round at the Ban Chang golf course, Darren walked into a bar some 50 yards from the Camel pub and restaurant and was immediately set upon by one of the semi naked "hostesses" who slowly removed her bikini top while sitting on his lap.

Several drinks later, they both disappeared upstairs for maybe half an hour, Darren returning with a big grin on his face.

Darren had just cracked his first hole in one in 15 years.

Darren began to enjoy his golf and began to play a couple of times every week, always choosing a golf group that were playing the Ban Chang course.

Lun began to become suspicious.

Darren had become much too happy of late and Lun hated Darren being happy.

Thai girls do not like their boyfriends or husbands being happy – it's a culture thing.

One day she told him that she was going to spend a week with her mother way up North in Chang Rai, and sure enough, 2 days later, suitcase in hand she climbed into a taxi on her way to the bus station.

As it was an all-night bus journey, Darren waited until the middle of the next day before he rang Lun, who confirmed that she had just arrived at her sister's house.

Cock a hoop, Darren rang his Ban Chang candy bar, and one hour later she climbed out of the taxi and walked into his house.

Skipping the preliminaries, it was straight to bed and Darren once again scored a hole in one.

The temperature was rising.

The candy bar's squeals, ooaa's, and yes, yes, yesses filled the room and found their way out onto the street via the open window.

Darren was just on the verge of completing the 18-hole course when the 45 inch, brand new smart TV came crashing down and connected with his head.

Lun hadn't gone to Chang Rai – Lun had barely travelled round the corner before climbing out of the taxi and was staying across the road at a friend's house in order to confirm her suspicions.

Darren was now semi-conscious and unable to move as Lun dashed into the kitchen and grabbed a carving knife.

I'm going to kill you both

The terrified girl grabbed her clothes, dashed out of the door completely starkers, and ran down the road pursued by Lun slashing at her with the carving knife, both girls screaming.

Darren meanwhile had come round and barricaded himself in the bedroom.

Darren's initial mistake had been a simple one that all serial fornicators are aware of – sadly, Darren was still a novice.

You must always take a shower after a round of illicit "Ban Chang golf."

A wife can smell another woman's perfume from several miles away, and when it is always the same perfume it becomes even more serious.

Thai girls can sometimes make a meal out of the slightest rule infringement, this one however will not be found in the rule book of The Royal and Ancient golf club of St. Andrews.

CHAPTER 26
BILL

We hadn't had the bar for long when one evening Rinda introduced me to Bill.

Now Bill was of a species that I hadn't previously encountered.

Bill thought that he was a ladyboy when in fact he had far more genetic commonality with an ape.

Bill was in fact distantly related to Rinda; probably related to a branch of the family that couldn't possibly have left the jungle canopy more than a couple of generations earlier.

Bill had no definable shape – Bill had hairy legs – Bill resembled a cross between a proboscis monkey and a Barbary Ape.

Bill's father

Bill was wearing a blue mini skirt, his face was covered in makeup and lipstick, which when coupled with his dyed multicoloured spiky hair, ape like shape and looks, would have provided a whole team of anthropologists with enough research material to last them a lifetime.

"Bill wants to work for us." said Rinda.

"Bill has more chance of becoming Miss World," said me. "Tell Bill to go away before he frightens the customers, and while you are at it, ring the local zoo and see if one of their exhibits is missing."

Bill left shortly afterwards in order to seek his fortune elsewhere.

A couple of weeks later I was at home watching the football when the phone rang. A rather worried Rinda informed me that Bill was again in the bar and was really drunk and threatening to eat one of the girls.

Perhaps 15 minutes later I arrived at the bar and politely asked Bill to leave, noticing that his lipstick and make-up were all over the place and he stunk of cheap Thai whisky. He refused, so I asked him again. He still refused, at which point I gently took him by the arm and told him to come with me as I had something interesting to show him.

As we approached the road at the front of the bar I smiled and spoke soothingly to Bill.

"If you go far enough to the left you will come to Pattaya Thai. If you go to the right, you will find Pattaya Klang. Your only other choice is to go forward, headfirst, straight under the Baht bus that is heading in this direction and you have 2 seconds to choose."

Bill scurried away towards Pattaya Thai and was never seen again or so it seemed.

I would guess that some 3 years had elapsed, when one evening, I walked into the bar and noticed Rinda in conversation with an absolute film star.

"This is Sophia," Rinda said. "Don't you remember her?"

I shook my head, there was no way that anyone would ever forget Sophia.

Sophia smiled and I positively melted.

Monty wasn't quite so impressed and hid deep within the recesses of my shorts.

I wondered why; Monty usually spotted a beautiful candy bar long before they came into my line of vision.

"The last time we met Billy darling, you were just about ready to throw me under a baht bus." Sophia's voice was perhaps a little husky and had a slight American inflection.

I nearly passed out as a mental picture of a proboscis monkey and a Barbary ape hybrid flashed in front of me.

Is that really you Bill?

Within weeks of disappearing, Bill had met a middle-aged American plastic surgeon who had fallen deeply in love with him – her – whatever, and whisked him off to his American clinic, where after extensive cosmetic jiggery pokery, he had somehow managed to turn him into Sophia.

The legs were slim and hairless, the bottom round and firm and connected to a waist so slim that I could have almost spanned it with my hands. The silicon boobs were magnificent, and the ape like face had been transformed into a highly sculpted piece of porcelain, with a slightly aquiline nose in place of the stubby Thai one that is found in certain regions. The high cheekbones exaggerated the beauty of the deep brown eyes.

Gone was the poorly bleached hair and crooked teeth, and in

their place was the sort of perfection that only lots of money can create.

OMG Bill - errr Sophia

I didn't have the heart to ask her if the crown jewels were still operational or whether they had also been lovingly transformed into something of far greater interest.

Monty read my thoughts and shook his head.

Somehow, he just knew the truth but for some strange reason he would never tell me the answer or how and why he knew.

The occasion had been my birthday party one October night at the Dragon bar, and I had left at 2 in the morning full of Tiger beer. Rinda got home at 6, knickers in her handbag and bra round her waist - maybe I left too soon.

During the party, some half a dozen ladyboys turned up which was quite surprising as the Dragon bar is usually a ladyboy free zone, and testicles in a skirt are quite rare there.

Nevertheless, their presence was quite welcome as they proceeded to buy me lots of drinks.

There is no such thing as a free meal, and so it came to pass that a few days later, Rinda commanded me to attend a birthday party of one of the ladyboys, and as she had another party to go to, I had to go alone - oh joy.

"Here's 1,000 Baht," she said. "Tonight you have to return the compliment and go to a bar called Delirious and buy the birthday "girl" a few drinks."

Ten o clock tonight found me at the bar sporting the only pair of testicles not wrapped in knickers and covered by a mini skirt.

Monty felt distinctly uncomfortable and had pleaded with Rinda to go to the other party with her, where he would feel much happier in the company of real women.

As instructed, I bought the "girl" a drink, and keeping my rear end firmly to the wall of the bar, watched in amazement as a steady procession of seriously gorgeous "girls" walked into the bar and began gyrating to the music being performed by the band outside the bar.

A film star called Jasmine bought me a drink.

Jasmine was gorgeous, as was "her" friend, Raya.

Suzy bought me a drink.

Suzy's friend, a tall blond beauty dressed in a skimpy bikini also bought me a drink.

A round of Sambucas followed and yet another round appeared, followed by several more.

Better looking than the girls sometimes.

This was turning into quite an evening as Raya put "her" arm around me and kissed me on the cheek, her breast full and enticing as they brushed against my chin.

The room was beginning to spin as yet more sambucas found their way down my ever-willing throat.

England was in lockdown and I was feeling not in the least bit guilty.

Suzy's hand wandered to a place that it shouldn't have.

With a flick, Monty knocked it away before I could respond and reality kicked in.

I was "alone" in a bar with only Monty for company, surrounded by some 30 stunningly beautiful "women", all of whom were fully equipped with lavish portions of meat and 2 veg - I didn't sign up for this.

I paid my bill and headed for the exit, running the gauntlet of multiple bottom pinching and goolie tweaking.

It wasn't really too unpleasant physically, but mentally, my sexuality had been tested to its limit; I may well now be suffering from a sexual form of PTSD.

I headed for the Dragon bar.

At least the knickers there covered what knickers were designed to cover.

CHAPTER 27
MR SPANKY

One beautiful sunny afternoon I was sat at my bar doing my main job, which is to ensure that all the Tiger beer that I sell is of the correct quality and at the right temperature. I take my job very seriously and spend hours at the task sometimes working my fingers to the bone, often into the early hours of the morning.

My other main duty, ably and willingly assisted by Monty, is to train my 40 Siren bar girls. I must confess that whilst being one of the most enjoyable jobs on earth, (after fishing) I have come to appreciate that being of a certain vintage I no longer have the energy of an 18 years old and must confine the training schedule to short, sharp sessions when Rinda is visiting family members somewhere up in her Thai jungle village.

Anyway, one afternoon, Monty and I were sat at the bar watching the world and an assortment of tits and teeth walk by when we were joined by Orbi and Granville who were on holiday from Atherton, my hometown in Lancashire.

How any parent could be so cruel as to name their son Granville is beyond me; I can only assume that they had badly wanted a girl and so named him Granville as a form of punishment.

After an odd beer or two, Orbi suddenly stood up, and waving to a guy across the road shouted "SPANKY, OVER HERE".

"Spanky?" I thought, now that's a strange name.

The gentleman in question crossed the road, walked into the bar, and shook my hand as Orbi introduced us both.

"Spanky, this is Billy Makin," Orbi said. "I was married to his sister Jean for 20 years."

"I remember Jeanie, Orbi, smashing little girl, adored a good spanking." Spanky slapped Orbi's bum as he spoke.

Orbi glared.

Spanky also hails from Atherton and he was not in a very good mood.

Where did the name Spanky come from?

You may well ask!

Spanky likes to spank girls, and while doing so focuses a video camera on their bare bottoms; then by selling the series of spanking videos on various internet sites makes lots of money in the process.

I can't really comment on either the ethics or the morality of his profession owing to my line of work. In my defence I have no control over what my bar girls get up to with my customers.

You might say that I simply run a dating agency that also sells beer.

The reason for Spanky's bad mood was that he had just returned from the police station having been on the receiving end of open wallet surgery.

The previous evening, Spanky, by way of a few bob had persuaded a local Thai bar girl to join him in his room to star in his latest spanking video, mentioning in passing the occasional key words of model and film contract. In reality, the only thing that ever matters to Thai girls is the money. All other promises are pointless and do not even enter the baked bean sized brain in their heads.

Offer them a fiver today or 50 quid tomorrow and they will snatch your hand off for the fiver.

The camera was set up, down came the knickers, and as the girl bent over his bed Spanky set about spanking.

Gentle
spanks
to begin
with

Now thanks to numerous experiences with Thai girls, Spanky spanks very gently to begin with, as on one previous occasion he had begun proceedings with an overly enthusiastic slap only to have the girl stand up and kick the living daylights out of him.

Take
that you
pervert

He gently rubbed the girls bottom and offered a few little pats.

So far so good.

He increased the tempo and patted harder.

The girl moaned with obvious delight.

Spanky began to spank.

Sometimes Spanky likes to use 2 willing girls

Strangely, there came none of the usual complaining. On the contrary, the girl yelped with obvious delight and encouraged him to really lay it on.

Spanky really laid it on, and soon his hand was on fire and he could take no more.

"Harder Spanky, Harder! – Faster Spanky, Faster!" The girl gasped between gulps of air. "Use the whip Spanky – Use the whip."

The girl urgently wanted more pain so out came the whip.

Use
the
whip
Spanky

Spanky the sadist had finally achieved his lifelong ambition of meeting and spanking a masochist.

Personally, I cannot see the pleasure that can be had by handing out or being on the receiving end of a good spanking. I've lived such a sheltered life and to find that such practices had taken root in the town of my upbringing came as quite a shock.

The question now of course is why was Spanky in such a bad mood having just filmed the spanking video to beat all spanking videos?

Well, the girl had gone home alone that evening, and the next morning she could barely get out of bed. She had hobbled down to the local police station, where in front of a dozen disbelieving coppers, she had dropped her knickers in order to show them the result of Spanky's handy work. Her poor bum was bruised black and blue and covered in a series of red welts from the whip.

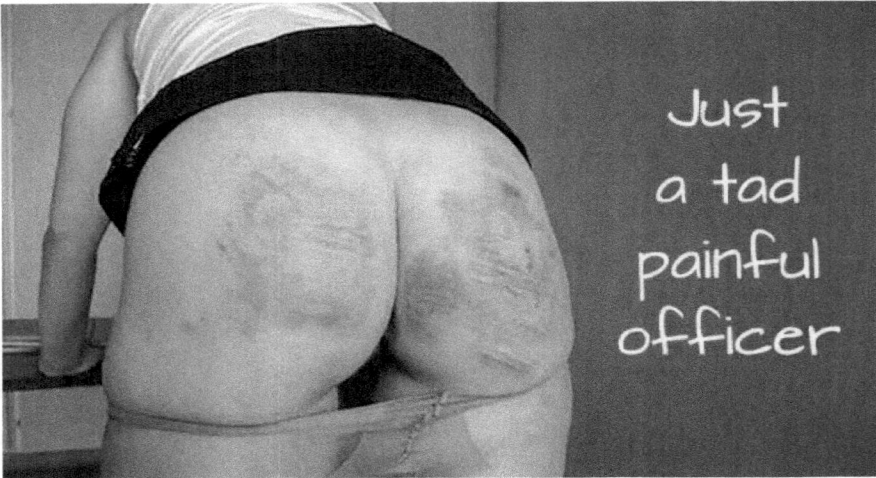

Just a tad painful officer

Spanky was duly arrested.

Thirty minutes before entering my bar, in front of the same dozen coppers, all of whom could barely stand up for laughing, Spanky had just paid the girl a bucket load of compensation rather than face a charge of GBH.

That was why Spanky was in such a bad mood.

So, if you quite inadvertently come across a spanking video to beat all spanking videos, whilst innocently browsing the internet of course, you now know where it was filmed and the man who filmed it.

It may be of interest to people of the same sexual persuasions as Spanky to know that I know the girl, and I have it on good authority that she still enjoys a good spanking; but whatever you do.

Leave the whip at home.

CHAPTER 28
DOES SIZE REALLY MATTER?

Having seen the transformation that Bill's plastic surgeon lover had achieved, I was beginning to believe that nothing in Thailand could possibly surprise me any longer.

Physically, I suppose that this is still the case, however, the ways and culture of the Thai girls still hold a certain fascination with their openness and their unpredictability.

A couple of years ago, my new young cleaner at Dragon Bar 1 asked me if she could sit outside with my bar girls when she had finished her jobs.

She was a small girl, barely 5 feet tall, cute rather than pretty and a little on the plump side.

As she was only 18 and straight from a jungle village in Isaan, the conversation was conducted through Rinda acting as interpreter, who then advised her to borrow some sexier clothes and a pair of high heel shoes from one of the girls and to ask them to show her how to apply make-up and stuff.

Rinda also explained what the job could possibly turn into if she was successful.

Her eyes lit up and she nodded excitedly.

This was indeed a gamey little girl.

A little
help then
go for
it girl

The next day, having finished her cleaning jobs, she came downstairs and took her place at the front of the bar with the other "hostesses", looking a million dollars from the frumpy little cleaner of the day before.

Not only was she gamey, but for some strange reason she seemed to hold a fatal attraction for my bar customers who couldn't wait to give her money and to explore and witness the carnal delights and techniques that she had perfected during her pubescent Isaan days with half the men and boys in the village.

Within a few months she had lost weight, learned quite passable English, and with both of her legs operating at full capacity had checked out the ceiling decoration of half of the hotel bedrooms in Pattaya.

Her favourite hotel

One day I had to be at the bar at 12 – mid-day for a little business, and 12-30 found me sat at the front of the bar checking the quality and temperature of the beer when my little girl turned up on the back of a motorbike, dismounted, and walked over to me.

This is now the conversation almost word for word.

BILLY — You're a little early for work today darling.

GIRL — Been with customer all night Billy.

BILLY — Good time?

GIRL — Great. We boom boom all night. I love my job, last night I so horny, I not have boom boom for 2 days. Man have velly big cock. I like big cock. I smoke (I'll let you work that one out) his cock this morning and we boom boom again 2 times.

I love my job

This conversation was becoming interesting and Monty was all ears having recognised the voice. Unfortunately, Rinda walked over so my little girl left and joined a group of girls who were applying their warpaint ready for work.

Monty swore.

Rinda glared at him.

From the oo's, aah's and laughter that I could hear from the back of the bar, it became pretty obvious where the conversation was going.

It's strange really, but in the many English pubs that I have drunk in, I honestly cannot recall any similar conversation with an English barmaid.

So – size really does matter then.

WELL, don't be so sure.

A year or so ago I was having a drink at Charlie's bar when Mr. G — joined us.

I had heard rumours of Mr. G—, and half an hour later as I stood at the gent's toilet, he came in and stood a few feet away from me.

I simply had to see if the rumours were true and threw a sideways glance.

I audibly gasped, as with both hands he wrestled with an out-of-control python that was threatening to strangle him.

Mr. G— had been born with 3 legs, only 2 of which had toes attached.

Monty immediately went into a deep sulk.

I mentioned this freaky phenomenon to Rinda later that evening, but positively refuse to type her verbal response as I had to hold her under a cold shower for half an hour before locking her in the bedroom for the rest of the night.

Why do I relate such a useless story then?

Well, a few days later, Mr. G— joined me for a drink at the Dragon bar, and as his Thai wife was up the jungle for a few days visiting relatives, he had decided to take his pet python for a walk in the hope of finding a mate for it.

He chose Legs, one of my most popular Eurasian girls, so called because her legs almost reach up to her armpits, and with a friendly wave in my direction took her back to his apartment to introduce her to his best friend.

I in turn visualized Legs turning up for work the next day sporting a big grin and walking with a slight limp.

Now why do I call her Legs?

I thought little of it until a couple of days later when Mr. G— again turned up at the bar.

On seeing him, Legs froze; she then screamed, ran upstairs, locked herself in her room and refused to come out until after he had left.

"What the hell is that?" said Legs

Mr. G— was to be disappointed that night, as Legs had told all my other girls about his pet python and no-one would go near him.

My little ex-cleaning girl was out with a customer that night, and on returning and hearing the story begged me to tell her which bar Mr. G— usually drank in.

So you see, once again size really does matter and sometimes it can work against you.

Don't you feel much better now ? Knowing that, or are you still sulking?

CHAPTER 29
STRANGER THAN FACT

There are times when running a bar here in Pattaya that you think that you have seen it all and suddenly you realize that you have barely scratched the surface.

Having lost my little cleaning girl, who on trying out the bar girl scene had turned the job into a lifetime dream and was now earning pots of money for doing what she enjoyed most in life, I now needed a new cleaning lady for both the bar and the guest's bedrooms.

"Leave it to me," said Rinda, and sure enough one of her relatives from the jungle village appeared a couple of days later.

I have mentioned before how Thai girls often look a good 10 years younger than their true age, well, the reverse frequently seems to happen when they reach middle age. A woman of 50 often looks 60 plus and so it was with Nan my new cleaner.

After a couple of weeks, Nan had finished her cleaning jobs one day and asked Rinda if she could sit at the front of the bar with the girls.

"Over my dead body," I said. "She will scare the customers and lower the whole tone of the place."

Rinda, subservient as ever, gave her the nod and the excited old battle axe disappeared upstairs to her room, returning some 15 minutes later dressed to kill and with make-up and lipstick that must have been applied in the dark with a trowel.

I disapproved and complained to no avail as she took her place alongside a dozen young tots who were either sat or standing outside the bar unsuccessfully trying to attract customers on what was a quiet day.

Imagine my surprise when within 5 minutes, Nan walked into the bar arm in arm with a decrepit old Pikey from Dublin, who then began buying both her and the rest of the girls a nonstop stream of drinks before bar fining Nan and disappearing with her in the direction of his hotel.

This continued for a whole week before the Pikey bought Nan out of the bar and set up home with her. Within a couple of months he had sorted out a date for their future marriage back in Dublin.

A future life of luxury for Nan

I was once again short of a cleaner.

What the hell do I know anyway?

* * *

One evening three Arab looking guys, perhaps in their late 20's/ early 30's, and their dad came into the bar. They were on holiday from Bahrain and seemed to have pots of money, and sure enough the girls clustered round them like money hungry flies around a honey pot. The 3 young guys soon sorted a girl each who sat on their knees and began consuming endless lady-drinks as the men drank Jack Daniels.

Their dad looked a little forlorn as none of the girls seemed interested in him, so Rinda walked over and sat with him.

I left the bar and went over to Charlie's bar so as not to be in the way, returning some 2 hours later.

The 4 guys had left taking the 3 girls with them and Rinda was sat at the bar with a big smile on her face.

"The old chap just offered me 50,000 baht just to go out for a meal with him," she said triumphantly.

"WHAT! Why didn't you go then?" I was in shock.

"He would probably have wanted to Boom Boom me." She was most indignant as she spoke. "What would you have thought if I had gone with a customer?"

"Why didn't you ring me then?" I shouted. "He could have bloody well kept you for 50k!"

Rinda's new wardrobe

A couple of times a year a millionaire businessman from Hong Kong travelled to Bangkok on business and always spent a few days in Pattaya, calling in most nights at the bar. He got to know Rinda quite well and took her phone number, always ringing her as he flew in so that she could ensure that his 2 favourite girls would be available for the duration of his stay.

Now this guy was seriously loaded and had bought a superb bungalow just outside of Pattaya for the 2 occasions a year that he stayed.

Just before Christmas a couple of years ago, he rang Rinda and asked her to "deliver" 5 of the prettiest girls that she could find to his house as he was having a 3-day party with his business pals that he had flown over with from Hong Kong.

Rinda was always well paid for sorting out the girls for him, so on the chosen evening, she delivered the "goods" to his doorstep and drove back to the bar a couple of hundred quid richer.

Home delivery service

A few days later, one of the girls re-appeared at the bar and began talking to Rinda.

The businessman had taken a particular shine to this girl and had only bought her a brand-new Toyota car for her 3 days of affection.

"Bloody hell." I said as Rinda told me afterwards.

She grinned. "He offered me a new Mercedes if I stayed for just the one night when I took the girls." she said.

"Why didn't you ring me?" I exploded. "He could have shagged me to death for a new Merc."

**Morality and fidelity come with a high price
tag; nevertheless he had found mine.**

CHAPTER 30
NUL POI

T'was half time at football on the TV in my bar one night when a stranger came and sat by me.

"Remember me Billy," he said. *"I was drawn next to you on the Thames at Wolvercote a long time back."*

I did in fact remember the day (It was indeed a long time back) as I only ever fished the Thames at Wolvercote once and had managed to win on the day.

"This is my first time in Pattaya Billy, and I've only been here for a couple of hours, so perhaps you can give me a little advice."

Not exactly being a Pattaya veteran, I looked at him questioningly.

"I'm looking for a girl Billy, not just for sex but for a serious relationship," he went on.

"Oh boy, here we go again." I thought. "Another lamb to be sacrificed at the altar of the Thai female loin."

Pattaya isn't that sort of city you must understand, everyone, and I do mean everyone falls in love within the first couple of days of arriving, often within the first couple of hours as there are no girls like Thai girls for massaging a man's ego or whatever else takes her fancy and comes readily to hand.

He then described to me the type of girl that he was looking for, as I in turn imagined myself as a judge at the Eurovision song contest mentally totting up the likelihood of his success using a score of one to ten.

"She must be pretty."

This was a good start as most of the 100,000 or so girls can be quite beautiful. The remainders however will be divided between the not too pretty, and the hung like a baboon, deep voiced type of girl, in fact, to be fair the ladyboys can be absolutely gorgeous.

5 points.

"She must be genuine and honest."

Nul poi — Rarer than rocking horse droppings.

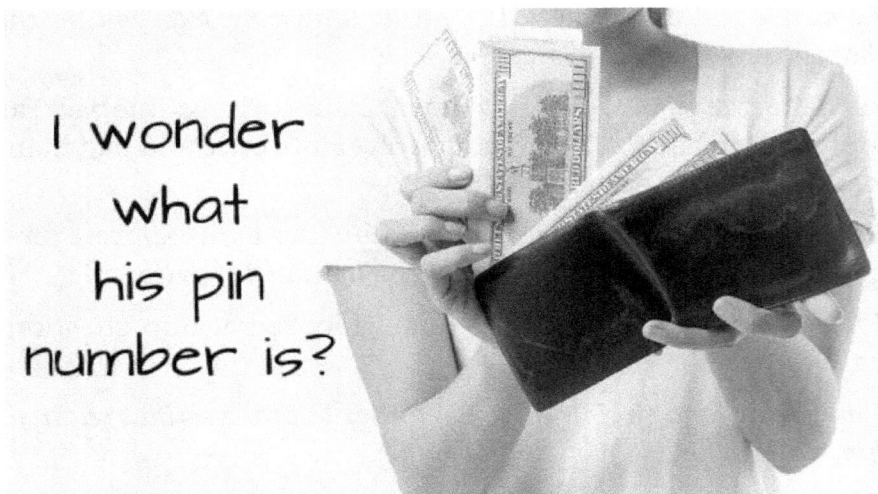

I wonder what his pin number is?

"She must not tell lies – I hate people who tell lies."

Nul poi — Do not exist on planet Thailand.

"She must not love me only for my money."

Nul poi — Why do you think that she is in Pattaya you plonker?

"I would like her to be a good cook."

Nul poi — This was perhaps a contentious one. Most Thai girls can use a microwave or fry up something that looks, smells, and tastes like buffalo dung, and is in fact the best laxative known to mankind.

"If I have to go back to the UK for a few weeks, I must be confident

that she will remain faithful."

I managed to keep a straight face, but Monty couldn't contain himself and the guy looked around to see who was laughing.

Nul poi — very Nul poi — infinitely high Nul poi.

I lonely
while you
away
Farang

Really ought to be a massive negative score.

The likelihood of finding such a girl in Thailand is on a par with being struck by lightning in a submarine at the bottom of the Pacific Marianas trench.

"She must be careful with my money."

He was perhaps onto a winner here.

She will indeed be very careful with his money, as she will send half of everything that he gives her to her extended family back in the jungle village, (this can number in the hundreds) then carefully hand the rest over to one of her many Thai boyfriends or carefully gamble it away.

Nul poi —

"Naturally, I would like her to be good at sex."

At last, this time he was onto a definite winner.

Sex is not only the all-consuming passion and obsession of every Thai bar girl, but also the recognised national sport of Thailand; the government pressing strongly for its inclusion in future Olympic Games.

Any potential suicide bomber would rather eat his explosives than find himself shagged to death in Paradise whilst on the receiving end of 72 Thai virgins.

Remember though, 72 Thai virgins would mean 72 prams and 72 sets of nappies.

Ten points.

By now I had heard enough and had decided that the nearest thing that he was likely to find in Thailand to HIS perfect woman – lived up a tree, ate bananas, and spent most of the day searching for fleas and scratching her bottom.

Visions of Duane's baboon relatives entered my subconscious.

LSD flashback

I of course was the lucky one, and as Rinda often checks my Facebook and computer work, I have to say that she scores a perfect ten on all counts.

Visions of both Adam and Mr Bobbit flashing before me as I type.

CHAPTER 31
A DOG'S DINNER

Around 3 years ago, Rinda and I were living at a lovely little site just past Pattaya Klang called Pattaya Chalets. It was a pretty oasis of green surrounded by high rise apartments and hotels and consisted of a dozen chalets and a small 3 storey block of single room apartments.

On the road leading into the site was a decent sized piece of land consisting of a small pond surrounded by an area of dense rushes, and living on the only dry bit of land were half a dozen stray dogs.

Pattaya has hundreds of such packs, all of which are fed daily by local Thai people, who being Buddhists will not kill anything other than each other.

One morning we walked out of the site to be greeted by 7 adorable little puppies. Their mother was wary yet allowed us to stroke and play with them.

The next day, same again, only this time there were 6 puppies.

Every other day one of the puppies disappeared until there was only one left, mother taking it to a grassy patch on the other side of the road.

The obvious assumption was that being so adorable, people were simply helping themselves and turning them into family pets.

It was perhaps 2 or 3 weeks later as I was walking back to the chalet in the early hours that the security guard began shouting at me and waving frantically as he ran towards me.

Bloody good job that he did as well, because slithering across the road was the biggest python you can ever imagine.

I adore man's best friend

Its head was in the grass on one side of the road and its tail was still leaving the swamp, its body easily as thick as the top of my leg.

I froze as it moved across the road a couple of yards in front of me.

I also noticed a large lump in its belly – no guessing what that was.

The puppies had been the Hors d'oeuvres and mummy was the main course.

Sure enough, the next day a poor little orphan puppy was wandering around looking for his mummy – he didn't last long.

Cruel as it may seem, without the snake the place would have become over-run by dogs, and with a never-ending supply of protein served up on an almost daily basis, the snake simple fed and grew without ever really needing to hunt or to leave his self-service swamp restaurant.

* * *

Thailand is home to a huge variety of snakes, many of them, like the cobra, being deadly poisonous, the strange thing however is how many still turn up in the towns and villages. Many of these snakes live in the underground drainage system and move freely around town un-noticed, munching their way through rats and any stray dog that crosses their path.

A couple of years ago the Thai press published the story of one such snake that took a wrong turn, its head appearing up through the water in the toilet of a private house close to Bang-kok.

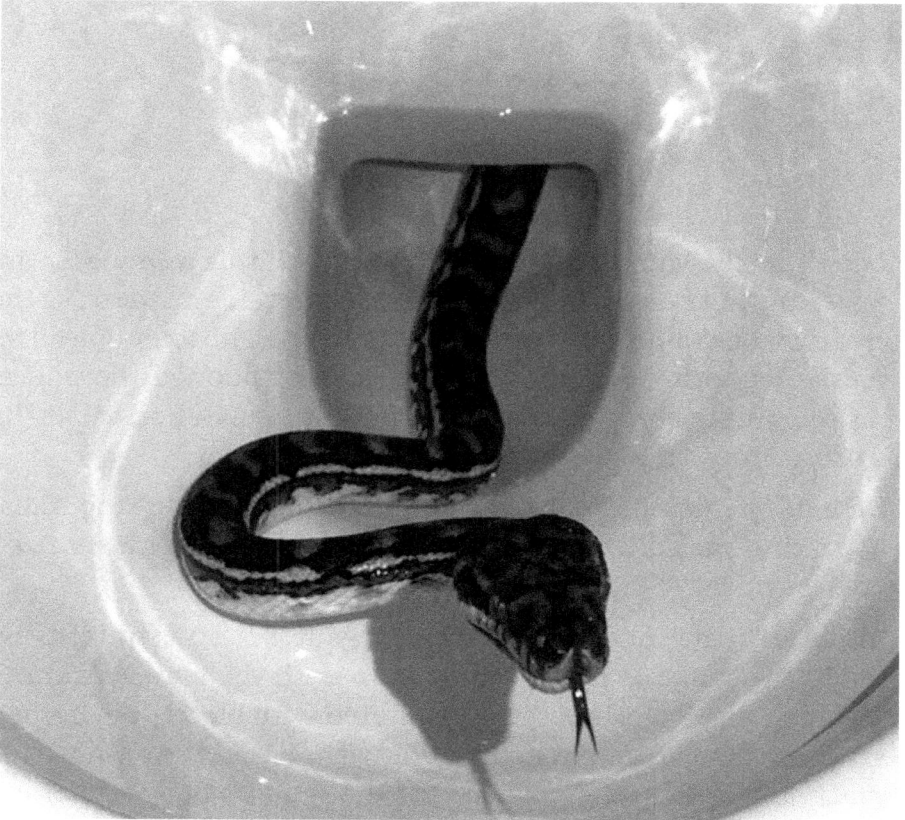

Unfortunately for the owner of the house he had just sat down on the toilet.

The snake looked up and seeing what appeared to be a clump of juicy morsels just in front of its nose, opened its jaws and clamped down hard on the poor man's crown jewels.

They look delicious

I don't really want to go much further with this as my eyes are watering, but being a Buddhist, the man's wife refused to cut the creature's head off no matter how much her husband pleaded, so she left him screaming in agonyas she phoned the police, his screaming being in a much higher pitch than normal as the snake clamped down ever harder.

He in turn held the snake's head with both hands to stop it disappearing back down the drainage system with his most prized possessions.

Along with the police came the fire brigade, both outfits refusing to kill the snake as it is illegal, and so with the man screaming and the toilet walls becoming splattered with blood, the firemen set about dismantling the toilet only to find that the python was much longer than they had at first thought, its body stretching several feet round the toilet bend and disappearing somewhere within the house plumbing, much of which had to be dismantled.

Eventually, after close on two hours of trying, the firemen managed to prize the snake out of the drainage system and force it to release its grip on the still screaming man's goolies.

Personally, if the snake had clamped its jaws round my goolies, I would have kept it alive and spent the rest of my life sticking hot needles into it.

The firemen released the still hungry snake back into a local drain unharmed.

Now you know why Monty always inspects the toilet carefully whenever I sit down.

Back into my time machine and moving back to my Singapore army days, for a few weeks I shared the cashier's office with a lovely chap called Colin who had an equally lovely wife called Sue.

Sue managed to get a secretarial job with BFBS, the radio station that catered for the forces based in Singapore and Malaya.

One day, Sue suddenly dashed out of the toilet into the office, knickers round her ankles, still peeing as she ran and screaming at the top of her voice in terror.

The DJ left his station mike on and ran into the office to see what the commotion was.

Half of Singapore island were now listening to what appeared to be someone being murdered.

Still screaming and peeing, Sue pointed at the toilet.

On checking out the toilet, coiled right above the DJ's head was a very big python, just about ready to throw a loop and drop onto him.

He ran out, joining Sue in screaming, (he was a poof) and several thousand people listened to their radios in absolute amazement at the sound of Sue and the DJ both having absolute hysterics.

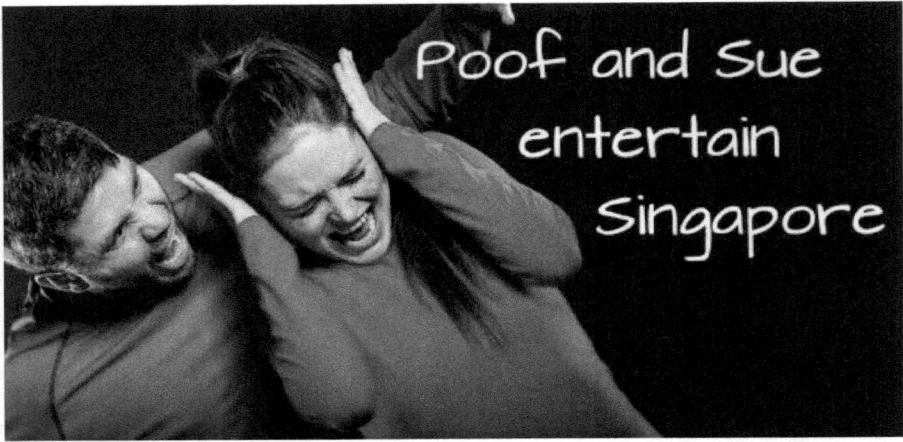

Poof and Sue entertain Singapore

There was to be no more BFBS music for the rest of the day as the police had to call in a special unit to remove the beast, having first received hundreds of reports of either a terrorist attack or mass murder at the radio station which completely overwhelmed the island's telephone system causing a complete shutdown throughout half of the island.

CHAPTER 32
WINGED ASSASSINS

Having originally flown to Thailand with the intention of playing lots of golf, I must admit that the best laid plans sometimes go astray when accompanied by a stubborn, single minded individual like Monty.

Monty has never liked golf, and after I have been therapeutically massaged between shots by a pretty Thai caddy, he purposely gets in the way of my swing at every possible opportunity.

Not only are the people of Pattaya an odd assortment of genders, but the golf bats themselves can trans morph into PMT influenced psychotic female clubs that display hormonal disfunction at the drop of a hat.

This phenomenon has often been discussed by members of the Sugar Shack golf society and appears to happen on a monthly basis as with most females.

I was having quite a decent round at the Mountain Shadow course one afternoon accompanied by a rather tasty candy bar caddy, (caddies are compulsory), when my driver suddenly developed PMT.

The ball shot way offline and disappeared into the rather rich foliage of a tree without seemingly coming down.

"Oh dear, oh dear, oh dear," I said to my caddy candy bar.

"No problem beeelly," she said. "I make feel better after finish, we go home together."

Now I have to admit that not only did she look the part, (definitely not assembled for working in the paddy fields), but her massage technique between shots was intentionally quite erotic.

You so good beeely

A vision of Rinda sharpening the knife in front of me and Charlie as we sat on my settee flashed in front of my eyes.

Monty abruptly returned to standby mode.

Still carrying my driver, I walked towards the tree leaving the caddy to walk in the opposite direction towards the golf buggy and then drive to catch up with me.

The ball was nowhere to be seen.

I looked up at the tree.

There came a strange buzzing sound.

What is that buzzing noise?

I was horrified to see that my ball had embedded itself deep into the hive of a swarm of giant Asian hornets and they were well angry with events.

Before I had time to move, they spotted the driver in my hand, and putting 2 and 2 together worked out that I was responsible for partially demolishing their home without even considering the possibility that my driver may have developed PMT.

The entire hornet army attacked in military formation, and soon I was legging it across the fairway surrounded by dozens of nature's predatory wonders, each one taking great delight in ramming the pointy bits of their red-hot arses into any part of my body that they encountered.

Monty shrunk into a target not worth bothering with and disappeared somewhere deep within the recesses of my loins.

Ahhhhhhhhh

The pain is instant and almost unbearable, and a single sting often causes death through anaphylactic shock.

I had multiple stings, and when I passed out on the course, they decided that I had been punished enough and flew back to their tree to effect a spot of DIY.

The journey home in the society bus was horrible, as stuck in traffic for almost 2 hours there was no way to get me to a hospital.

Rinda picked me up at the Sugar Shack bar as the bus arrived and having only recently taken out a rather large insurance policy on my life, she decided to skip the hospital and let me die at home to save on the medical bills.

I didn't die, much to Rinda's dismay, and she had to cancel the order she had just placed on a new car.

The only thing that died was the golf driver.

When I began to recover a couple of days later it was executed and is now in 4 pieces and stuffed in my redundant golf bag.

I haven't played since nor do I intend doing so.

Monty has finally convinced me that Pattaya offers far more attractive and interesting forms of exercise than golf.

CHAPTER 33
NO-ONE EVER LISTENS

While in many ways Pattaya may well seem like heaven on earth to people used to the strictures of Western society, it does however have its do's and don'ts.

Thai bar girls, while blessed with all the physical attributes necessary for an enjoyable stay in Pattaya, forgot to turn up on the day that brains were being dispensed, and instead they stood in the queue that was dishing out tempers and violent tendencies.

The late John Wilson, (bless him) who was living in the South of the country at the time, told me of a chap that he knew, who after a particularly violent argument with his Thai wife of 8 years, went to bed that night and woke up dead the next morning with his throat cut.

I hadn't had the Dragon bar long when I was invited to a wedding reception at the Elephant bar next door.

The Thai bride got a little drunk and stepped too far into the road, being slightly caught by a passing motorbike taxi.

The poor man stopped to make sure that she was OK, only to be attacked by the girl, knocking him off his bike. As he tried to cover up from the attack, the groom, a big Dane, saw what was happening and instead of pulling his new wife away went over and punched the motorbike taxi man.

At this point, I must mention rule 3 in Thailand – never get involved in an argument or a punch up with a Thai man or woman.

They operate under a different set of rules to the Western World, and for them to lose either a fight or an argument is to lose face.

Perhaps 15 minutes after the trouble I was back in my bar when all the guests from the wedding reception dashed in leaving the Elephant bar empty.

The Great Danish plonker who had punched the motorbike taxi man was now barricaded in his room upstairs, while stood outside was the Thai man randomly firing his gun through the bedroom door.

Try to remember rule 3, especially with the bar girls.

They can be extremely volatile and go from nought to ten on the anger scale in a fraction of a second without even going through the gears.

I had to get rid of a cashier called Emm a couple of years back for attacking customers, also including me on one occasion. The problem always happened when she had been on the receiving end of several drinks, usually bought by the customer that she then attacked.

Now Emm most certainly hadn't turned up on the day that they handed the brains out, and one day demonstrated this in spectacular fashion.

The occasion was Big Buddha day, and everywhere had to close at midnight and remain closed for the next 2 days.

No-one, including the supermarkets, could sell any alcohol.

I walked into the bar mid-afternoon and could barely move for crates of beer.

"What the hell is this lot Emm?" I said.

"Me velly clever Billy, wholesaler he close for 2 days so I order stock for 3 days. Me not stupid."

"But Emm," I said. "The bar is also closed for 2 days."

Emm paused and adopted a blank expression for around 30 seconds before speaking. "Me not think of that Billy – me stupid."

I nodded.

* * *

Emm really wasn't any more stupid than most of the cashiers that have worked for me, and Noisi, the one that I have at the moment working Dragon 2, has an IQ that is definitely in the negative and would come second in a direct mastermind competition with a newt.

After buying the bar our first job was to redesign the place in order to make it look like Dragon 1.

We had all the electrics disconnected and placed the 3 necessary electrical boxes in a safe place in a cupboard, these being for the TV, the internet, and the security cameras.

My bird brain cashier decided to do a spot of tidying that evening, noticed the boxes and threw them in an outside bin.

It cost 50 grand (baht) to replace them.

Even though Noisi has been doing the job of reserve cashier at Dragon 1 for a couple of years now, she still needs the calculator to work out the change from a 100 baht note if the bill is 90 baht. If it was 99 baht, the calculator would still be pressed into service.

Thais are not wired up the same as Farangs, and one cashier at a friend's bar took possession of a 100 baht note for an 80-baht bill. She punched the figures into her calculator and hit a wrong button. The astonished customer then held out his hand as she passed over 920-baht change.

The ability to use any form of logic or common sense appears to have bypassed Thai bar girls.

Still, Monty doesn't seem to be too interested in their mental abilities, he much prefers their more physical attributes.

I suppose he does have a point.

CHAPTER 34
THE BALLAD OF THE MISSING BRAIN CELL

When I first arrived in Thailand some 8 years ago, I became enthralled and fixated on an ancient legend that has been around in the country for hundreds of years.

The wise old sages tell the story of the first people to set foot in the country, and of how on the day that God handed out brains, the Thai contingent were still fast asleep in bed, and when they eventually turned up, only one brain cell was left - a quiet, shy little rascal that had been hiding in the corner of God's celestial box of goodies.

The ballad and myth of the missing brain cell was born, and the story is told throughout the land to remind all Thai people of their superiority above all other races.

Anyone married to or living with a Thai girl will confirm this unchallengeable superiority.

Centuries have come and gone, and despite worldwide attention and the best technology that the Western world has at its disposal, the missing brain cell has eluded all attempts of capture to the point that there are now people who even doubt its very existence.

Scotland has its Loch Ness Monster.

Islam has its winged horse.

Christianity has its Santa Clause.

America has its Big Foot.

But Thailand?

There can be little doubt that somewhere among its 60 million inhabitants, a brain cell exists.

I firmly believe that it does despite all evidence to the contrary, even though I have yet to meet the first Westerner who agrees with me.

Thais are not particularly gifted in the brains department, and it is not uncommon for a Thai girl to ask for 5,000 baht just to take her out of the bar for a meal. Most of them will settle for 1,000, but to the unsuspecting tourist, he may well feel that 5,000 is the going rate.

Many of the Agogo bar owners are equally stupid and greedy, and in certain establishments ask for 1,000-baht bar fine instead of the normal 3 or 400.

This stupidity and lack of brains seems to permeate all levels of Thai society, resulting in a population that does not need Google, as every Thai knows everything and will never listen to any form of reasoning whatsoever.

This is what is known as losing face and is far more important than life itself.

One night, for the umpteenth time, I witnessed the stupidity of the Thais first-hand.

A ladyboy who worked for me complained to Rinda that a customer had refused to pay "her" for services rendered - - don't ask.

Rinda asked me to have a word with the customer in question as he was at a local bar, so I popped over to see what was wrong.

Now this guy is a pretty wealthy bloke, an Austrian solicitor who regularly takes out ladyboys - - to each his own.

The going rate is between 1 and 2,000 baht, however this chap always gives the "girls" 20,000. Don't ask me why.

My ladyboy did whatever lady boys do and then demanded that he pay her 20,000.

He would have done voluntarily, but to be met by what was almost an ultimatum, resulted in him telling her to push off. That was why he paid her nothing, and in my opinion quite rightly so.

Even though I fully agreed with the bloke, Rinda did not, despite being very intelligent for a Thai. There was no way that I could get through to her that sheer greed and stupidity by the ladyboy had just cost her 20k.

It was of course the Farang's fault - never ever the Thai.

Back to losing face again.

No Thai will ever admit to having made a mistake.

I collected the originally agreed 1,000 baht from the laughing customer, handed it to the ladyboy and ushered "her" through the door – permanently.

CHAPTER 35
A PASSION REKINDLED

Rinda had been stuck up the country for months because of the damned virus, and Monty was becoming restless and putting on weight through lack of exercise.

I had to get him out of the house to give him a little fresh air; why not go fishing, I thought.

I mackled up a few bits of coarse tackle that I had brought over with me from Tenerife and spent a few bob at a local tackle shop and I was on my way.

My first port of call was a local fishery that a friend had recommended, and before setting up my tackle, I ordered breakfast at the fishery.

Two menus arrived.

The first one was full of pictures of the various dishes to be eaten, and the second one was also full of pictures of dishes, only these dishes were all in their early 20's, very beautiful, and instead of a price list contained only phone numbers.

"If you get bored with catching fish," said the fishery owner. "Give one of the girls a ring and she will be round in 10 minutes or so. You can use the chalet by the lake for 300 baht."

Monty abandoned all thoughts of fishing and fresh air and reached in my pocket before passing me the phone.

I had run my Wolvey fishery back in England for 20 years and had never thought of such a wonderful addition to the angler's enjoyment for one minute.

The day was pleasantly hot and as Monty soaked up the afternoon sun, my mind drifted back to my days running the fishery.

I had received a phone call from a young lady from the water vole society asking my permission to use my fishery for a study of what at the time was becoming an endangered species.

I met her at the fishery one morning and took her for a walk around, wondering why such an attractive young totty was engaged in sorting her way through water vole turds when the field alongside the fishery was full of long, sweet smelling grass, and was out of sight of the anglers.

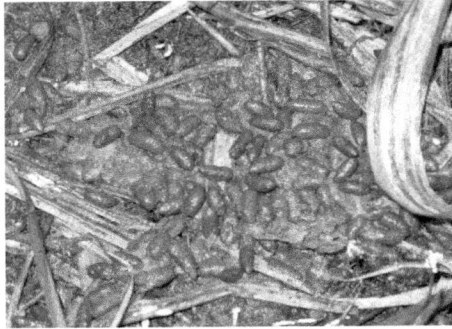

The excitement began to mount

With the discovery of each pile of vole turds, she became more and more excited, culminating in what appeared the be a life changing sexual experience on discovering what she thought may well be an otter turd.

I resisted informing her that the life expectancy of any otter that appeared at the fishery was considerably less than my life expectancy when walking round the streets of Tehran with a shirt bearing the message "Mohammad likes pork chops".

I gazed longingly at the long grass but to no avail. The "otter turd" had got there first and continued to titillate her sexual bits for the rest of the afternoon.

Her eyes rolled with ecstasy as she informed me that she had discovered the biggest breeding water vole colony in the midlands, possibly the country.

I was so excited.

Around 2 weeks later, she phoned me and informed me that together with the rest of the vole turd gathering fraternity, it had been unanimously agreed that I would shut down the fishery for one month in order to allow the voles to breed in peace.

I pointed out that if it ain't broke - you shouldn't really try to fix it.

"I can enforce that decision by law", came the response.

"And I can ban you from my private property, I can also remove the mink traps from the river that runs through the site and shoot and poison every vole on site if I want to", was my reply.

The fishery remained open, and I allowed her to return to continue her turd gathering the following week.

A victory of sorts.

She arrived, her demeanour being so meek, compliant, and vulnerable, that I had to ply her with a few glasses of wine at the local pub as an acceptable form of foreplay.

It worked a treat.

We then headed for the fishery in a state of feverish excitement.

The bloody farmer had cut the grass the day before, so we spent a wonderful afternoon collecting vole turds.

Ah well.

CHAPTER 36
JOKER OR NUTTER

As anyone who knows me will tell you, I have always been a bit of a bugger for practical jokes, sometimes perhaps going a bridge too far.

As I wrote in my book Fishing and Testicles, the time that I emptied more than a drop of Chrysoidine maggot dye into the office coffee jar almost caused a bigger fuss than the Kung Flu virus.

Half the office, the coffee drinkers, turned fluorescent canary yellow, and the works' nurse was heard screaming over the phone in blind panic at someone on the other end in the local hospital.

The same chrysoidine dye ended up in a neighbour's sock that was on the washing line, and the poor sod became convinced that he had got gangrene in his foot.

Anyway, one particular day didn't start off too well.

Rinda rang in order to tell me that she would probably be stuck in Corona virus isolation some 700 miles away in the Golden Triangle for maybe a month or two, as Chonburi, our region, was going into lockdown and no-one would be allowed to enter.

Great, my sanity was already a little suspect, and it wasn't going to take a lot to push me over the edge.

I had no milk, so after a shower I slipped on a pair of shorts, t shirt, and flip flops, and made my way to the 7/11 store all of 100 yards away, forgetting to wear my face mask.

The security guard waved and pointed to his mouth.

I mouthed – sod off.

The chap and two girls outside the apartment that provide the motorbike taxi service looked disapprovingly at me and pointed to their mouths.

I again mouthed – sod off.

The girl at the 7/11 stepped back, pointed to her mouth, and refused to serve me.

I once again had to run the gauntlet of the motorbike taxi man and women, and the site security guard before I finally arrived at the lift to my apartment in order to grab a mask and repeat the whole process before I could have my morning cup of coffee.

Stood outside the lift was an oriental chap, his wife, his teenage daughter, and a wizened old lady who I guess would be his mother.

They glared at me, pointed to their masks, and the chap faked a spit and said something in chimpanzee that was almost certainly abusive.

Not being in a particularly good mood by now something snapped.

Sitting on a table next to the lift was a bottle of hand sanitizer.

Insanity kicked in.

I took off my tee shirt, grabbed the hand sanitizer and began to cover my entire body with squirts of liquid, before proceeding to rub in the mess all over my body, including my hair, paying particular attention to the bits beneath my shorts.

Monty objected strongly.

The four Orientals stood open mouthed in disbelief.

It was when I handed his daughter the bottle, turned around, and asked her to rub some into my back that the punch up almost started.

I suddenly felt much better, so I slipped on my T shirt, collected my mask, and merrily made my way back to the 7/11 store where I bought a bottle of milk.

Self-isolation does however have certain advantages.

I have begun to have long philosophical discussions with myself and have yet to hear one single dissenting voice among the one of me regarding my sometimes slightly racist, slightly xenophobic, slightly chauvinistic, slightly misogynistic, slightly homophobic, slightly Islamophobic, middle of the road views on life.

"What a night last night Billy." Kevin said as he joined me in my bar for a noggin or two. "I've been trying to pull this film star down at the Champagne Agogo for weeks and last night I finally cracked it."

"Good night then kiddo?" I said. "Expensive?"

"Not too expensive but it didn't exactly go according to plan, in fact it turned into a complete disaster."

Kevin then went on to tell me that occasionally, his sexual performances weren't perhaps up to scratch.

"I get too excited Billy." He said. "Sometimes I finish before I even get started."

"Oh." I said. "Perhaps you should try doing it under a cold shower."

"Last week," he went on. "A mate who also suffers from premature ejaculation told me about this cream that they sell at all the local pharmacies, so I bought a tube with the instructions to rub it into the end of my dick before performing."

I was now quite intrigued.

"Anyway," he said. "After spending a fortune on this film star and plying her with drinks for most of the night, I finally got her back to my place."

It was now my turn to become excited.

"We both got undressed and that was when I remembered the tube of cream. I went into the bathroom and rubbed a great dollop on the end of my dick and climbed back into bed."

"Go on - go on - don't stop now."

"Well, that is where the problem started. Instead of the usual kissing and a bit of petting, she immediately disappeared under the clothes and......

"Oh my god!" I said. "Go on."

"After about half a minute of heaven, she let out a gasp, jumped out of bed and dashed for the bathroom shouting "OOH OOH UGG UGG. She couldn't speak a bloody word. The cream was a local anesthetic and all her mouth had gone numb just as if she had been to the dentist."

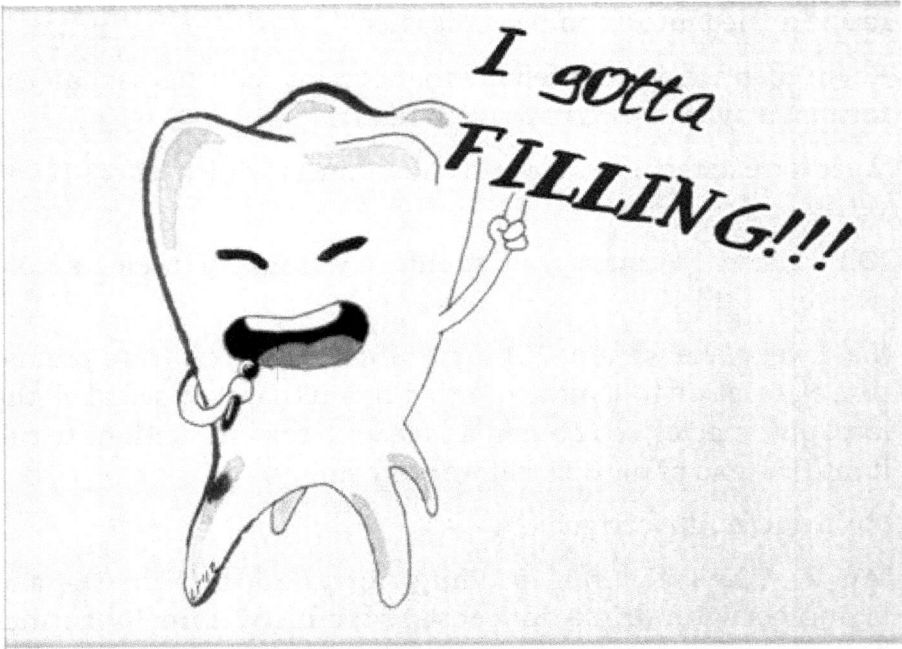

"And then?"

"She screamed "uck ouuu, uuu astard", got dressed and went home. I don't think I will be seeing her again somehow."

"Did the cream work then Kevin?" I ventured.

"Uck ouuu, uuu astard." He replied.

CHAPTER 37
THE MEANING OF LIFE

Do you ever just sits and wonder how you got here?

I don't mean in a Darwinian sense but more of why me, why here, and why now situation, when life could have taken you in a thousand different directions.

I had such a philosophical moment recently at my bar.

Geoff, Rinda, and I had just left a birthday party, been hijacked by Adam at Fubar for a couple of noggins, and I was now sat on my own at Dragon bar.

Rinda was talking to a couple of girls who were desperate for a job, Geoff was up to his neck in bar girls and fighting for breath, and I was in pensive mood pondering the meaning of life.

Laid out in front of me like kippers on a fishmonger's slab, were 17 of my girls, ages ranging from 18 to 30, a sort of selection box of Cadburys chocolates, each one with its own unique flavour, shape and outer coating, and each one ready, willing, and able to be consumed without the worry of being too overloaded with calories.

Delicious and low in calories

How on earth did I get here?

Why was I here, now, at my time in life when I could be in a thousand different places?
Surely there must be more to life than beer, cigarettes, and mucky women?

Pattaya sometimes gets you like that.

This box of Dragon bar chocolates is always temptingly in your line of vision, begging you to try just the one; to carefully take off the wrapping paper and admire the craftmanship of the chocolate alchemist, to gently lick the outer coating and let the sensual, pheromone laden manna from heaven slowly dissolve in your mouth, knowing that beneath the delicious outer layer is the mythical yet shortly to be sampled forbidden fruit of the gods.

Slowly, as the beer began to take effect, the 17 girls began to blur.

Their shape changed, morphing into something even more pleasing to the eye.

Seventeen plump perfectly formed, and exquisitely decorated trout began to emerge through the alcoholic haze.

The meaning of life became crystal clear.

I was born to fish.

"Are you missing me Billy?"

Rinda was still up't country with members of the Bangkok Girls Mafia, a shadowy outfit comprising of the class of 1999 at her Bangkok university. In rotation, the group travel the country renewing old acquaintances and memories, before moving on to the next member.

"Are you really missing me Billy?"

"Yes darling, I am really missing you."

The voice sunk an octave and exhibited sexual undertones.

"What are you missing the most Billy?"

"The car, I have to use a taxi to go fishing."

She tried a different approach, still retaining the deep, husky, sexual inflections.

"What would you most like me to do when I come home, Billy?"

"The washing up, I'm running out of plates and the sink is full."

Really missing you darling

Midnight now as I type this, middle of the afternoon in a normal Pattaya before the plague, and I have been instructed to inform everyone that Rinda is now selling all beer at the Dragon Bar for 55 Baht.

"Why not do a 2 for 1, I suggested?"

"They cost too much to buy." Came the reply.

"I didn't mean the beer; I meant the girls. One fat one and one slim one for the price of one, maybe one pretty one and one ugly one for the price of one?

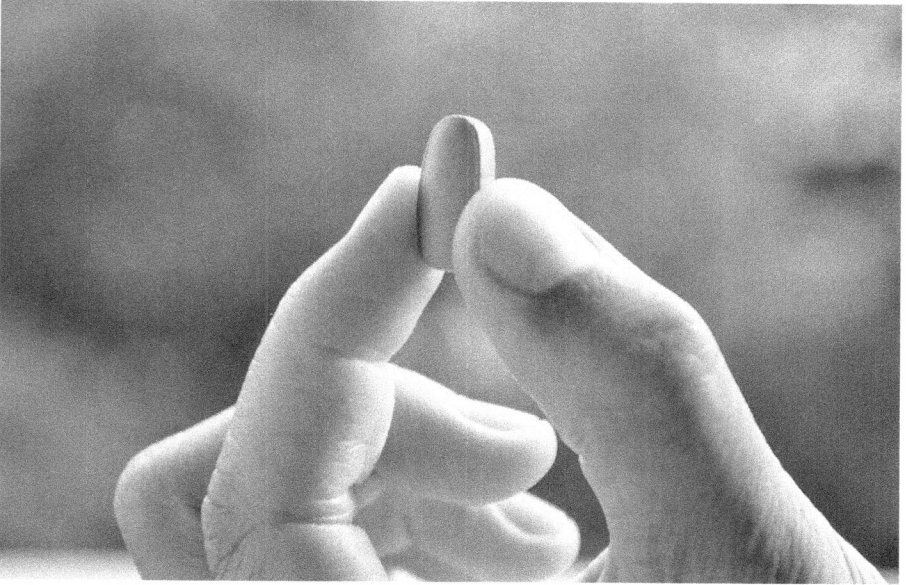

We could even offer a free Viagra tablet with every bar fine.

"How about if I offer to video every performance, maybe even join in. (I could feel Monty nodding his approval) We could make money by selling the videos on the internet, possibly even a little blackmail if we know their wives."

Rinda glared at me. They don't seem to have a lot of business sense these Thais, so 55 Baht a bottle it is.

CHAPTER 38
END TIMES

And so the journey through a dream like fantasy period of life must be brought to a close.

Adrenaline charged recklessness must be replaced by quiet, unassuming domesticity.

Monty must accept that he is no longer 18 and be put out to pasture.

Pipe and Labrador must replace alcohol and pit bull.

Loving wife must replace nymphomaniac candy bars.

All night carousing must be replaced by TV and a hot cup of coco.

LIKE HELL IT WILL

MONTY IS STILL IN THE SADDLE

Beer tastes better than ever.

My time clock has gone into reverse and I am heading both willingly and disgracefully back in the direction of my 18-year-old youth.

Together with Rinda and Monty, I now run two Pattaya bars and my third life is well under way.

Welcome to Pattaya.

The Sex Capital of the world.

Will I ever go home?

How can I?

Monty has hidden my passport.

Monty's fantasy finally fullfilled forever.

Or is it?

Coming soon..

BIGGER TITS and TEETH in THAILAND

WOULD YOU PLEASE CONSIDER LEAVING A REVIEW?

Just a few short words would help others decide
if this journal is for them.

Visit www.amazon.com and your "Orders" page where
you can leave your comments and thoughts.

Best regards and thanks in advance.
Billy Makin

◆ ◆ ◆

BOOKS BY BILLY MAKIN

JIHAD 1 – The lost scriptures

JIHAD 2 – A bride for Allah

JIHAD 3 – In the name of the prophet

JIHAD 4 - The Final Solution

THE LIGER SYNDROME

O'MALLEY – The wrong package

THE SMILING PILL

REINCARNATED

Teenage books

THE AMAZING ADVENTURES

OF SPOTTY SPINDLE

Comedy Books

TITS and TEETH in Thailand

FISHING AND TESTICLES

Fishing Books

THE GOLDEN YEARS

◆ ◆ ◆

THE AUTHOR

An authentic and archetypal 1950's baby boomer.
Working class roots, with standards and values that evolved in the grim, dark satanic mills and coal mining towns of the North West of England

Grammar school and university educated.

Soldier, engineer, and entrepreneur.

Designer and creator of Europe's largest ever commercial fishery.

Left England for sunnier climes at the age of 50, whilst still retaining UK consultancy work.

Now living in Thailand, where together with his Thai wife, he runs two successful businesses in the entertainment industry.

Still writing for various UK publications.

Between bouts of fishing and beer appreciation, Billy Makin writes books, acquiring a rapidly expanding fan base and becoming recognized as one of the UK's most exciting novelists.

"Is the earth really round"...

BOOKS BY BILLY MAKIN

JIHADA 1 – The lost scriptures
JIHADA 2 – A bride for Allah
JIHADA 3 – In the name of the prophet
THE FINAL SOLUTION – Beyond 1984

THE LIGER SYNDROME
O'MALLEY – The wrong package
THE SMILING PILL

Teenage books
THE AMAZING ADVENTURES
OF SPOTTY SPINDLE

Comedy Books
TITS and TEETH in Thailand
FISHING AND TESTICLES